Parallel Paths to Constructivism

Jean Piaget and Lev Vygotsky

Parallel Paths
to Constructivism

Jean Piaget and Lev Vygotsky

by
Susan Pass

INFORMATION AGE
PUBLISHING

80 Mason Street • Greenwich, Connecticut 06830 • www.infoagepub.com

#55044604

Library of Congress Cataloging-in-Publication Data

Pass, Susan.
  Parallel paths to constructivism : Jean Piaget and Lev Vygotsky / by
Susan Pass.
       p. cm.
  Includes bibliographical references and index.
  ISBN 1-59311-145-2 (pbk.) – ISBN 1-59311-146-0 (hardcover)
  1. Piaget, Jean, 1896–Contributions in education. 2. Vygotskiæi, L.
S. (Lev Semenovich), 1896-1934–Contributions in education. 3.
Educators–Biography. 4. Education–Philosophy. 5. Constructivism
(Education) I. Title.

  LB775.P49P37 2004
  370.15'23–dc22

                                                          2004009776

This book is dedicated to Jesus, my God;
Edward, my husband;
and Jan, Suzy, and Michael, my children.
Without their help and love, this work could not have been done.

CONTENTS

THE UNITY OF DIVERSITY
AND THE DIVERSITY
OF UNITY

Since its origin, scientific thinking has never been restricted by any kind of time frame. By its very nature, scientific thinking represents an intellectual wholeness, and becomes the property of humankind. Herein lies the source of its constant development.

The development of scientific psychological ideas is determined by the aggregation of many factors such as cognitive, social and subjectively-personal. It has its own logic of development which is expressed in the gradual change of scientific paradigms, approaches and methods of research into psychological reality. A confirmation of this is the phenomenon of so-called "parallel discoveries" when contemporary problems arising from the constant development of psychological knowledge and based on previous discoveries are addressed simultaneously by scholars representing different scientific schools and traditions, at times very distant from each other. The work of the Swedish scientist Piaget (1896–1980) and the Russian psychologist L. S. Vygotsky (1896–1934) is a clear example of such an occurrence.

In her monograph, S. Pass wrote about these two outstanding psychologists of the 20th century who brought a tremendous input into the development of contemporary psychology.

Parallel Paths to Constructivism: Jean Piaget and Lev Vygotsky, pages ix–xii
Copyright © 2004 by Information Age Publishing

The basic methodology of Pass's book on the work of Piaget and Vygotsky is a synchronous comparative approach to the study of the history of psychology. The same method was brilliantly used by the Soviet psychologist Ananiev when he studied the history of Russian psychology. It permits a new look at well-known facts and historical events of scientific knowledge. It opens the window to the comprehension of psychological reality by the human mind. Pass gives an opportunity to discover the communalities and peculiarities in the development of psychological knowledge in different countries in the same period of time, as reflected in work of the scientists mentioned above. From this point of view, Pass's book serves as an example of the correct and constructive use of the possibilities of cross cultural simultaneous strategy in the study of the history of psychological science.

Of great interest is the elucidation of what unites the work of Piaget and Vygotsky and wherein lies the originality of their views and approaches. Because the whole paradox of the development of their thoughts is that, while working simultaneously and independently of each other on the same psychological problem, (the rules and stages of development of a child's psyche) they essentially came to completely different conclusions. Both these scientists proposed their own original view of the problem and developed well-founded and convincing conceptions from a scientific point of view which became part of the treasure store of world psychology. This again confirms the non-linearity, variety and multi-dimensionality of the development of psychological cognition.

The huge study undertaken by S. Pass has facilitated the clarification of a multitude of intersecting lines in the life and the work of the scholars examined. The detailed and meticulous comparative analysis of the biography of these two scientists, their lives and their scientific ideas, has allowed Pass to create a unified mental space of the creative work of these psychologists, to trace the logic of their thoughts, and to classify and refine the "deformed knowledge" about which the methodology and epistemology of science says so much. This is the main accomplishment of her research.

It should be noted that while working on similar scientific problems, Piaget and Vygotsky were following their own independent paths. As similar as their lives and work were, one can see at the same time drastic differences in their scientific point of view. Starting from the same ideas, (the acknowledgement of the role of speech in the process of formation of human cognition, internalization as the main mechanism or assimilation of cultural values of humanity, the egocentrism of a child's speech as a gradual stage of development) they were building their own perception of the process of forming and functioning of cognition and speech, formation of common ideas, rules of development of the psyche and mechanisms of learning.

For Piaget, the human mind is a natural product of evolution. It helps to find equilibrium within the environment and helps one to adapt to different conditions of life. Therefore, Piaget considers the development of the mind as a biological process. It has its own sources, rules (stages, sequences and so on…) that are developed as the result of the constant transformation, and socialization of natural and biological mechanisms. At the same time, socialization is defined as the foundation of the development of psychological functions; as a process of "humanization" of the psyche, biological in nature, and imposed from outside without an initially egocentric intellect. Correspondingly internalization is treated as a "rotation in" of the external forms and methods of interaction with the environment, its transformation into an ideal plan—plan of consciousness that is emerging through a sequence of different stages of intellectual development. Piaget shows this as the result of the development of personal experience of the child: in his treatment the individual remains at one with the environment. Education, while considered an important factor in this development, at the same time cannot change its development. It is predestined, given in the first place by the inner rules of psychological development.

Vygotsky considers both the human psyche itself and its development, not as products of biological evolution but as a result of the acceptance of cultural-historical experience of humanity by the child resulting from the interaction with adults. The psyche of the child is determined initially as a social factor and only later does the internalized social factor becomes a part of his nature. It becomes as a psychological mechanism that regulates the behavior of the child. Accordingly, education is not only a factor, but also an essential form of development. This is exactly the reason why Vygotsky constantly emphasized that the whole purpose of education lies in the organization of the child's interaction with adults and, if this factor is missing, then no development of the child can take place. Education as the foundation of development can play a double role—"Lag at the end of development " i.e., go behind development, adapt to it, exploit it or it may anticipate the evolutionary stages of development. The idea of "developing education" consists in the establishment of education that is going ahead and stimulating psychological development ("a good education is such an education that runs ahead of development and leads it").

The most vivid differences in these two scientists' point of view are in the treatment of egocentric speech of a child. Piaget considered it as a transitional stage from natural individual speech to social speech, i.e. as a form of socialization. From his point of view, egocentric speech is an, as yet, undeveloped form of communicational speech. For Vygotsky, egocentric speech is a form of origin and early beginning development of the inner dialogue. The development of the child's speech begins not from egocentric speech but from speech directed to adults. Of course, this is primitive, unstructured and incoherent, but it is not a reason to not consider it "real" social speech (as Piaget did). Vygotsky considers the process of the formation of speech as a transition from social speech to individual speech. He considers it as an inner psychological instrument for the regulation of the psyche that is the most important stage in the development of a child's thinking, his consciousness and psyche as a whole.

Similarities and differences in the approaches and views of Piaget and Vygotsky are a manifestation of the natural path to comprehending the truth, characterized by alternatives and variations. Without the multiple faces of unity and the unity of the multiplicity, science itself would lose its completeness and constructiveness.

Susan Pass's work, based on the model of J. Piaget and L.S. Vygotsky, convincingly and substantively demonstrates that comprehending the nature of the psyche is of a complex and dialectic character, and that one and the same problem may have varied denouements. This explains why an integral picture of the psychological cognition is possible only on the basis of a consideration of many different ideas, concepts, and theories represented by the history of psychological science.

As a perspective, a comparative study of the problems of Piaget and Vygotsky is given by the expedient entry into the Piaget-Vygotsky dialogue by the French psychologist P. Jane. His idea is that the development of the mind and complicated forms of thinking originate under the influence of real life problems that each individual solves while communicating with other people. This idea received an original interpretation and further development in the works of Piaget and Vygotsky.

The originality used by Pass in comparing the cross cultural approach in the work of famous scientists, the depth and the meticulous analysis, the range and the multi-dimensionality of research material, the importance of theoretical communication and practical conclusions make her work distinctive in the history of psychology and psychological science as a whole. There is no doubt that we await further ground breaking work in the future from Pass.

—V.A. Koltsova
(University of Psychology of the Russian Federation, Moscow)
—Y.N. Oleynik
(Moscow Humanities University, Moscow, Russia)

INTRODUCTION

No two people were more responsible for the current way lessons are taught worldwide than Jean Piaget and Lev Vygotsky. The impact of their thoughts on how a person learns led to lesson theories on how a person should be taught—starting in the last century and continuing today. Jean Piaget's genetic epistemology concentrated on the individual in learning. Lev Vygotsky's cultural–historical theory concentrated on the social in learning. All over the world, teachers today use each man's ideas. Some use them at different times in their classrooms and others have learned to use them combined into the same lesson—bringing us to the crux of this book; namely, there are many lessons to learn by discovering the dynamics in the lives of both men. While both were from very different countries, there are many similarities in their lives. While most professors teaching introductory educational psychology courses focus on the difference in their pedagogies, there are some remarkable similarities between their lesson theories.

Indeed, the communications that both men had with each other can lead a psychological historian to speculate on a combined pedagogy (i.e., the science of guiding a child) that both would have developed had their communications been allowed to continue—instead of being stymied by Stalin's repressions. In addition, both men overcame adversities that would crush others. How they did this provides a strong lesson either for those struggling with adversity themselves or trying to help those who are. Finally, this book will look at the origin of each man's main ideas that formulated genetic epistemology and cultural–historical theory. All of the points that

Parallel Paths to Constructivism: Jean Piaget and Lev Vygotsky, pages xiii–xviii
Copyright © 2004 by Information Age Publishing

will be addressed in this book are based on the premise that psychohistory is a legitimate method of research.

The people, ideas, and the strains of the chaotic 20th century profoundly affected Jean Piaget's and Lev Vygotsky's thinking. No two countries were more dissimilar in the 20th century than Piaget's Switzerland and Vygotsky's Russia. Yet, despite this, their personal biographies have uncanny similarities. Looking at their biographies leads one to observe the origin of the major ideas that formed Piaget's genetic epistemology and Vygotsky's cultural–historical theory. In addition, their respective biographies show how these men were able to conquer adversity in their lives (Piaget endured a dysfunctional family and Vygotsky endured a dysfunctional country) and the means by which they did so made them empowered to create their pedagogies that had a tremendous impact on education worldwide. Finally, both Piaget and Vygotsky (despite Stalin cutting off all east-west communications) tried to send their work to each other. When they succeeded, both changed their ideas in light of the other's statements. Projecting this process, it is possible to create a new, combined pedagogy.

I believe that the similarities in their personal lives (Chart 1) made it possible for their ideas to also have similarities. Researchers bring to their work not only their research efforts but also their backgrounds. It is their backgrounds of personal experiences that influence the scope and sequence of their research. Those wishing to expand the foundations of education should look more into how a researcher creates pedagogy. It is my belief that each man's pedagogy is subject to analysis not only by its ideas but also by the backgrounds or personal lives of its creator.

PREMISE

Both Jean Piaget and Lev Vygotsky encountered challenges at an early age. These challenges included psychological and physical disabilities in addition to social adversity. Piaget had two nervous breakdowns during his youth, a father who was cold and distant, and a mother who was mentally ill. Because of her "neurotic temperament" (Piaget, 1953, p. 238), his parents' marriage and subsequent family life were "somewhat troublesome" (p. 238). Not close to his two sisters and lacking any close friends his own age, Piaget relied on older mentors and solitary study to survive and, then, empower himself to create genetic epistemology.

Vygotsky was born a Jew in Czarist Russia. Periodically, the Czars would authorize persecution (i.e., pogroms) of the Jews. Vygotsky encountered two violent pogroms in his childhood: one occurred when he was only 5 years old (Pinkus, 1988). The other occurred only 3 years later (Dobkin,

1982). This last pogrom was so violent that Vygotsky's own father, Semyon Vygodskya, took up arms to defend his family and neighbors. For this, Semyon had to defend himself in court. Although Vygotsky's parents had a happy marriage and home life was pleasant, Vygotsky had to deal with persecutions and overt prejudice until the Russian Revolution. Vygotsky, like many Russian Jews, saw Lenin as liberating because they were given some freedoms (e.g., being allowed to live outside the Pale of Settlement and having the quota system eliminated for university entrance). Vygotsky, however, did not see Stalin as liberating and became involved in passive resistance after Lenin died. When Stalin became head of the USSR, Stalin killed many people. Vygotsky became a victim of such a purge. In addition, always of slight frame, Vygotsky became ill with tuberculosis in 1918. That debilitating disease killed him in 1934, while he was trying to defend himself in such a Stalinist purge.

Lesser men might have succumbed to these physical and environmental problems. Lesser men would have failed to reach their own potential. Both men developed coping mechanisms to overcome the adversities that they faced, which will be explained in this book. Also to be explained is how Jean Piaget and Lev Vygotsky used their coping mechanisms to start researching how children develop intellectually. Again, how they did this is discussed in this book with the premise that those coping mechanisms were the germ of creativity that led them to create their unique lesson theories.

Their coping mechanisms allowed them to turn their own personal difficulties to their own intellectual advantage and both were idealists who wanted to help others. The way in which these coping mechanisms operated resulted in publications that took those pedagogies worldwide, and these would have an initial and diverse impact upon American education. Initial, because they were put into classroom use immediately and, diverse, because the pedagogies were taught as exact opposites of each other: Genetic epistemology was seen as focusing on the value of individual learning and cultural–historical theory was seen as focusing on the social aspects of learning. This book will argue that there are actually many similarities in their respective pedagogies. However, the lesson that these two men bring to empowerment is found not only in their concepts, but also in their lives. Piaget and Vygotsky were both excellent examples of servant-leaders and this concept will be discussed in Chapter 6. I believe that, for the good of others, all people should strive to be servant-leaders.

By the time both men started their professional careers, they had already formulated their ideas and tested them successfully during their postgraduate jobs so that, when they arrived at their respective institutes (the University of Neuchatel in 1925 for Piaget and Kornilov's Experimental Psychological Institute in 1924 in Moscow for Vygotsky), they were able to spend the rest of their careers doing formal research and publishing—the results of which brought them to the pinnacle of their field.

TERMS

For the sake of clarity and information, terms used in this book are defined below.

Egocentric Speech. This is babbling. Piaget thought it would lead to mental illness and should be avoided as soon as possible. Vygotsky thought that it was part of the learning process.

Equilibration and Internalization. Piaget believed that equilibration is a set of processes that coordinate cognitive development in the individual's search for "true" equilibrium (Gredler, 1997). "Equilibration is similar to Vygotsky's idea of internalization" (Steffe & Gale, 1995, p. 510; Hamilton, 1997). Vygotsky termed internalization to describe the processes of cognitive development that a person goes though to understand something (Gredler, 1997).

External Speech. This is talking and both Piaget and Vygotsky endorsed it; although, Vygotsky said it was a tool of learning and Piaget would not agree to endorse that perspective until after Vygotsky died.

Internal Speech. This is talking to oneself. Originally, Piaget was against it. Later, he read Vygotsky and agreed with him that it was part of the reasoning process and should be allowed.

Optimal Mismatch and Scaffolding Scaffolding is very "similar to Piaget's idea of the optimal mismatch" (Kuhn, 1979, p. 356). In Piaget's idea of the optimal mismatch, a classroom environment is set at the highest challenging point for a student's chronological stage of development so that, with effort, a child can move, if the child successfully internalizes the problem through equilibration to the top of that child's stage of development (Hamilton, 1997).

Scaffolding is a term that was not used by Vygotsky, even though Vygotsky conceptualized the idea. It was first used by Jerome Bruner (1967) to describe a student being brought from the bottom of his stage of development to the top by a caring "social other" through the use of communication.

Stages of Development. Just as Darwin charted the development of species, Piaget wanted to chart the development of human cognition. He postulated four stages of chronological development, which are: sensorimotor, birth to $1\frac{1}{2}$ years; preoperational, from 2–3 to 7–8 years; concrete operational, 7–8 to 12–14 years; and formal operational (older than 14 years) (Gredler, 1997). Vygotsky originally postulated three stages of development; namely: precausality, secondary differentiation, and differentiation (Vygotsky, 1929). After reading Piaget and writing the Russian translation of the introduction to Piaget's Language and Thought of the Child, Vygotsky divided his first stage of precausality into two parts. In short, Vygotsky's precausality became primary differentiation and real instrumental. Now, Vygotsky had four stages of development: primary differentiation, real instrumental, secondary differentiation, and differentation (Kozulin, 1991).

Zone of Proximal Development (ZPD). The difference between the knowledge a child can obtain on her/his own and the knowledge that a child can obtain with the help of a "social other" (Gredler, 1997; Vygotsky, 1934/1984).

PERSPECTIVE

In the 20th century, no two countries were more opposite than Piaget's Switzerland and Vygotsky's Russia. Part of each man's struggle was the milieu of his country and his century. Piaget would forever be a product of Swiss democracy's fostering of individualism, and his genetic epistemology reflects that individualism. Vygotsky devised his cultural–historical theory to reform a dysfunctional nation, and nations are social creations. Perhaps it is because of the dramatic differences between their nations that many researchers focused on the differences between their two pedagogies.

In conclusion, while differences in their families and countries were obviously significant, the two men differed surprisingly little in their pedagogical views and their basic ideas. Their similarities in views and ideas are due to the similarities in their lives. Chapter 1 looks at those similarities by looking at influences in their childhood. Chapter 2 observes their adolescence. Chapter 3 concentrates on young adulthood. Chapter 4 covers their postgraduate work. Chapter 5 traces the origins of their major ideas. For Jean Piaget, we look at the origin of chronological stages of development, the role of language, the role of the teacher, optimal mismatch, equilibration, error, and play. For Lev Vygotsky, we look at the origin of zone of proximal development, internalization, stage of development, "the social other," role of language, error, sociohistorical context of learning, scaffolding and play. Chapter 6 deals with how Jean Piaget and Lev Vygotsky were able to overcome adversity and the lessons that can be learned by such overcoming. Chapter 7 provides a new pedagogy based on the communications that Jean Piaget and Lev Vygotsky had with each other, noting the influence such communications had on their mutual ideas.

It is hoped that the reader is willing to accept the idea that, within dissimilarities, similarities can be found. Knowledge of the biographical similarities between Piaget and Vygotsky sheds light on the similarities between their ideas. Both continued to care about the well-being of others until their deaths. Their lives, actions, and ideas reflect this concern. This concern forms the major trait of a servant-leader and that trait began its formation in their childhood.

CHAPTER 1

CHILDHOOD

INTRODUCTION

There are many similarities between Piaget and Vygotsky in their personal lives. Both were the oldest sons in their families. Psychological research indicates that the oldest child in each family is born with a proclivity toward leadership (Rothstein, 1998).

In addition, both were born in 1896. Both were exposed to authors who would influence their ideas while in childhood. Both wrote their first work at 10 years of age. Both underwent their faith's rite of passage (i.e., confirmation and bar mitzvah) within 2 years of each other. Both started elementary and secondary school at the same time. Both used their childhood extracurricular activities (i.e., outside of school) to explore the ideas that will form the basis of the respective pedagogies starting at 10 years of age. Both endured personal crises in 1911: Vygotsky's home was invaded during a purge and his father was tried and acquitted of defending that home and Piaget had a crisis of faith that would lead to hospitalization at Leysin, Switzerland.

As children, both Piaget and Vygotsky were considered child prodigies of sorts. Three glaring distinctions—one intellectual, one physical, and one social—would mark them from birth. Primary evidence attests to their gifted but troubled minds. These torments came from adverse situations within their childhood. Nevertheless, from early childhood, both showed a voracious, intense appetite for learning. After learning their letters, both became readers with intense concentration. While still children,

Parallel Paths to Constructivism: Jean Piaget and Lev Vygotsky, pages 1–20
Copyright © 2004 by Information Age Publishing

both started serious study of their first academic fields of inquiry, namely, natural science for Piaget and literary analysis for Vygotsky. Their knowledge of these subjects made them noted authorities by the age of 10 (Dobkin, 1982; Piaget, 1966a). Both knew that the path to success lay not with physical achievement but within their minds. Both sets of parents evidently approved of and indulged their sons' studies and both parents' position within their town encouraged the sons to seek their mark in academic venues.

By the time he was age 10, Piaget was a published author, assistant to the curator of the local museum, and invited to become the curator of another museum—until those wishing to hire him discovered his age (Piaget, 1953). By the time he was age 10, Vygotsky had helped his father save his family from certain death in a Czarist pogrom and wrote two essays plus one article (Dobkin, 1982). These would become the foundation of his doctoral dissertation, "The Psychology of Art."

By the time Piaget was 16 years old, he had become a dedicated mallacologist (or student of shelled animals) and noted author. In 1922 Piaget's mentor and the head of the local museum of natural science, Paul Godet, died, but Piaget

> knew enough about this field to begin publishing without help (specialists in this branch are rare) a series of articles on the mollusks of Switzerland [, which] afforded me some amusing experiences. The director of the Musee d'histoire naturelle of Geneva, Mr. Bedot, who was publishing several of my articles in the "Revue suisse de Zoologie" offered me a position as curator of his mollusk collection. (Piaget, 1963, p. 108)

Vygotsky further demonstrated his intellectual bent by organizing and leading various plays, debates, and lectures in his hometown before he was 16 years old. In fact, he became so knowledgeable on language and literary works that he was called "the little professor" by the time he was 17 (Levitin, 1982, p. 4). These acknowledgments of obvious genius and motivation were first acquired in nurturing, small-town environments.

HOMETOWNS

Piaget and Vygotsky were both born in the same year, each in a small town that displayed a nurturing environment for its youth, and each to families in which failure was not an option. Piaget was born on August 9, 1896, in Neuchatel, Switzerland. Neuchatel is the capital of a Swiss canton (e.g., province) and located on the French border. French refugees fled to Neuchatel at the time of persecutions against French Huguenots during the reign of the Bourbons and during the 1848 bloodless revolution that ousted Napoleon III. Some of Piaget's ancestors (and many of his neighbors) were among those refugees.

Vygotsky was born on October 24, 1896, in Orsha, Byelorussia. It was a small town not far from Minsk (Wertsch, 1985). His daughter, Gita Vygodskaya, says that when her father was born, Russia was on the old Russian calendar, so October 24, 1896, was actually November 5, 1896. His parents moved to Gomel, a somewhat larger town in Byelorussia when Vygotsky was just a little over a year old.

Both Piaget's Neuchatel and Vygotsky's Gomel provided a close-knit, homogenous society that encouraged intellectual pursuits and provided an environment where children could soar to reach their full potential. Both were homogeneous when it came to religion and social class. Gomel was a Jewish, bourgeoisie town that was the cultural center of its region. Neuchatel was a middle-class Protestant town that was the academic center of its region. Located within it was the University of Neuchatel, where Piaget's father taught and from which Piaget would graduate. Both towns had inhabitants who remembered religious persecutions and revolutions. The loss of lives that these events caused perhaps made them more nurturing and protective of their children.

Neuchatel, or Jean Piaget's Hometown

Most of the citizens of Neuchatel were French-speaking Protestants who encouraged a basic, middle-class conservatism. Neuchatel embodied the "stiffness and conformity of a prosperous and self-confident middle class active in a striking number of philanthropic, religious, social and cultural associations" (Vidal, 1994, p. 11). Neuchatel, a Protestant town, was on the French border about 60 miles from Geneva. "But the young Piaget was not in any sense Genevan. His roots were in Neuchatel" (Vidal, 1994, p. 1).

In 1848, there was a bloodless revolution in France that ousted the Napoleon monarchy. Many French Huguenots fled to Neuchatel during the subsequent persecutions in France. Many royalists also fled to Neuchatel. Neuchatel became prominent during Piaget's childhood as a center for social improvement. Its late 19th-century Protestant bourgeoisie tended to pursue "good works" and Piaget became part of that movement, thanks mainly to his mother. Piaget remained a Christian socialist until his second mental breakdown. He then became, like his father, an agnostic. World War I and Stalin's later reign of terror would cause Piaget's neighbors to change from liberal to conservative, but most kept their Protestantism.

Neuchatel was larger than Gomel. It had a population of 134,014 in 1900 and lay in western Switzerland on the northeast corner of Lake Neuchatel. It was and still is the capital of the canton bearing its name. When

Piaget was born, Switzerland had been a republic for half a century. But national unity was a fragile idea. French-speaking Switzerland worried about the dominance of German-speaking Switzerland. A Swiss-French Union was then formed in Neuchatel to defend and preserve the local French and Latin culture against Germanic infiltration.

This tension between the two groups of Swiss citizens increased during World War I and led to civil disobedience and demonstrations. The Swiss army occupied several cities in November 1918 during a very large general strike. Piaget witnessed this occupation because he was in Zurich doing postgraduate work at the time. Nevertheless, the cultural atmosphere of French-speaking Switzerland "was outstandingly rich" (Vidal, 1994, p. 13). Piaget's parents, especially his father, contributed to that richness (his mother cared for prisoners of war during World War I and his father was one of the town's published intellectuals).

Gomel, or Vygotsky's Hometown

Gomel was located within the Pale of Settlement (an area in Russia to which the Czar restricted all Jews to live, with the exception of Jewish lawyers). Winters were long and cold there. Thus, cultural events where one could forget the harshness of the environment were welcomed. Vygotsky's parents moved there because it was more of a cultural center than Orsha, where Vygotsky was born. Both parents wanted more for their children than Orsha offered. "Gomel was a relatively small town but one of the liveliest within the Pale" (Dobkin, 1982, p. 24). Both parents enhanced Gomel's culture with their philanthropic contributions and volunteer work—and Lev's father protected it during the pogroms. Vygotsky would later model this and become a cultural leader himself. Although he never directly stood up to oppression, he did emulate his father's courage by indirectly opposing Stalin. Risking his life, Vygotsky continued to communicate with the West. Stalin wanted to purge Soviet thought from "corrupting" Western influences and targeted Vygotsky. Vygotsky became a victim of a purge trial and was working on his defense when he died of tuberculosis.

Gomel suffered two pogroms during Vygotsky's childhood. Roving bands of bandits attacked Gomel several times during the Russian Revolution and caused much damage. What remained after such rampages the Germans completely destroyed during World War II. This included all personal records, letters, and pictures of the Vygodskaya family. Because so much about Vygotsky disappeared, it is said that to write about Vygotsky is "still to write about a figure half in shadow" (Daniels, 1993, p.15). Minority groups undergoing long stretches of persecution must become close-knit and nurturing to survive. The closeness that the Jewish town of Gomel had encouraged Vygotsky to develop his theory of the zone of proximal development (ZPD) and "social other" (Vygotsky, 1934/1984).

Conclusion

The nurturing found in the closeness of their homogeneous hometowns aided both men to reach their full potential. Help was also available from their parents. Even if Vygotsky's parents had a happy marriage and Piaget's did not, both sets of parents cared about their offspring.

PARENTS

Both Piaget and Vygotsky had challenging youths. As boys, they struggled to overcome handicaps that threatened to bar them from the adult roles they later played. As already explained, Piaget was born with a nervous constitution and was subject to several nervous breakdowns. Vygotsky's handicap was that he also had a weak constitution and was eventually afflicted with tuberculosis. Piaget suffered from a dysfunctional family and Vygotsky suffered from a dysfunction country.

From their parents, both learned as boys the advantage of a good defense. Jean Piaget's mother was put on trial for slander and Lev Vygotsky's father was put on trial for defending his family during a pogrom, when the attackers actually got inside the house. In both cases, the parents won acquittal. The skills that they picked up as boys were vital if one wanted to promote a new pedagogy. For each youth, the strongest outside influence toward overcoming his handicaps came from social relationships.

Jean Piaget was the first child and only son of Arthur and Rebecca Piaget. He had two younger sisters, Madeleine and Marthe. Lev Vygotsky was the second child and firstborn son of Semyon and Cecilia Vygodskaya. In 1920, Lev would change his name to Vygotsky "because he believed that his name derived from the village of Vygotovo where the family had its roots" (Dobkin, 1982, p. 24). Vygotsky had two daughters. Because they were not certain that the family really came from Vygotovo, the daughters, Gita and Asya, would return to their grandparents' surname.

Just as both hometowns were nurturing environments, so also both sets of parents did their best to nurture their offspring. Both sets of parents also contributed to the culture of their respective towns. Piaget's father wrote a history of Neuchatel and was a respected professor of medieval literature at the local university. Some of his colleagues and friends became Piaget's mentors (such as Arnold Redmond). Piaget's mother was active with the local school board and in obtaining humane treatment for prisoners of war.

Vygotsky's parents established Gomel's library. "The Vygodsky family was among the most cultured in the city" (Dobkin, 1982, p. 24). Vygotsky's father, Semyon, was an executive of the United Bank of Gomel and defended that town effectively during a czarist pogrom and, thus, saved many lives. His mother, Cecilia, encouraged literary and philosophical discussion groups with friends and neighbors. As civic leaders, Vygotsky's parents set up ZPDs (the difference between what an individual can accomplish independently and what the individual can accomplish in conjunction with another, more competent person) all over town—an example that Vygotsky would copy many times himself. Grateful to his parents (and unlike Piaget), Lev had them live with him in Moscow until their deaths. They all shared a one-room apartment in the basement of Kornilov's psychological institute with Lev's wife, two daughters, four of his unmarried sisters, and his older sister and her husband. "The room was very cramped," recalled Vygotsky's oldest daughter, Gita (Vygodskaya, 1994/1996, p. 1). When he grew up, Lev took care of his parents in their old age.

> Lev Semenovich loved his parents very much; he would show great respect to his father and he would be without fail tender, attentive, and helpful to his mother. I do not recall that we would address her using any other word than mamochka [mom]. When his father died he put all of the responsibility for the family on his shoulders and surrounded grandmother with even more attention, making sure that all the doctor's orders were strictly observed. (Vygodskaya, 1994/1996, p. 2)

Among both sets of parents, the mothers practiced their faith more than the fathers did. It was the mothers that insisted their sons go through confirmation and bar mitzvah. Jean Piaget's father was an agnostic and Lev Vygotsky's father was a Jewish free-thinker. Nevertheless, both fathers agreed to their spouse's insistence that their offspring go through their religion's rites of passage. Thus, Piaget would attend confirmation classes and become confirmed in his Calvinist faith in 1915, even though it would cause his first nervous breakdown. Vygotsky would have a bar mitzvah, even though he did not practice his faith actively after the Communist Revolution.

In his 1966 autobiography, Piaget wrote that he had to believe in the Protestant catechism, but he could not believe that the "Five Proofs for God" were true, given his scientific experience at Neuchatel's Museum of Natural History. The conflict between the logic of science and the faith of theology caused him to completely break down (Vidal, 1989). Lev Vygotsky "received a traditional Jewish education, reading the Torah in Hebrew, delivering a speech at his Bar Mitzvah, and so on. The rather frequent references in his work to the Bible can be understood in this context"

(Dobkin, 1982, p. 4). Both mothers, despite their own strong ties to their faith, would allow their husbands to introduce their sons to philosophy and free thinking. The talks and readings by their fathers played an important role in the formation of their children's mentality. The introduction by their fathers to the great philosophical writings led both sons to eventually work in educational psychology and how this happened is part of the scope for the rest of this chapter.

Thus, the picture that emerges from information about their early upbringing was that both sets of parents managed to create an intellectually stimulating life, grounded in both faith and ethics, but also allowing freedom of the mind. Despite persecutions or mental illness, both sets of parents saw to it that their sons would be given the tools to prevail over adversity.

FATHERS

Both fathers were similar in personality. Both fathers enjoyed reading philosophy and introduced their sons to Kant and Hegel. Both fathers were hard workers and were successful within their fields. Intellectuals, both fathers modeled successful scholarship. Both fathers were well educated and highly intelligent. Both fathers were leaders in their towns; Piaget's father was an intellectual leader and Vygotsky's father was a cultural leader. Both fathers, however, had a negative side to their personality that the sons adopted. For example, Jean Piaget's handwriting showed "traces of inherited causticity [severely critical]" (Duplain, 1913). In addition, Lev Vygotsky inherited a dark "fatalism" (Blanck, 1990; Dobkin, 1982; Vygodskaya, 1994/1996) from his father that had just as much to do with his father's bitterness as it did with persecution of the Russian Jews.

Piaget's Father

Jean Piaget's father, although a highly respected citizen of the town of Neuchatel, was no foreigner to controversy. Arthur Piaget was born in a town close to Neuchatel called Yverdon. He was the son of Frederic and Marie-Adele Piaget. His mother was American and his father was a French royalist. Arthur graduated from the gymnasium, or the European version of the American high school, in Lausanne, Switzerland, in 1884. Educated in medieval literature, by the early 1890s, he was a well-known Romanist. In the mid-1880s, he studied in Paris at the Sorbonne. There, he met and married Rebecca Jackson. In 1889, they left for Neuchatel, where Arthur became chair of Romance languages and literature at the University of Neuchatel. Showing his inclination for pugnacious words, Arthur proved that the *Canons' Chronicle,* the most revered document of Neuchatel's history, "was an eighteenth-century forgery" (Vidal, 1994, p. 13). This demonstration in his inaugural address displeased conservatives, gave rise to passionate debates, and won him a government appointment as state archivist in 1897. But it also earned him enemies that felt he had hurt their town's reputation; so, within conservative circles in Neuchatel, Arthur was considered difficult to get along with (Vidal, 1994).

Piaget remembered that his father was "not afraid of starting a fight when he finds historic truth twisted to fit respectable traditions" (Piaget, 1953, p. 237). Furthermore, Arthur "made some people unhappy for sentimental or political reasons" (Vidal, 1994, p. 14) when he critiqued the work of a local historian, delivered his lectures on the 1848 French revolution, and wrote about the University of Neuchatel's history. His criticism often extended to his personal relationships.

This tendency may explain his caustic words to his son about his son's first scholarly works. Arthur Piaget was "a man of painstaking and critical mind, who disliked hastily improvised generalizations" but who also taught his son "the value of systematic work, even in small matters" (Piaget, 1953, p. 237).

When he only 6 years old, Piaget invented an automobile (called an "autovamp" because he gave it a steam engine) and quickly rushed into his father's study for approval. Most parents would be proud that someone so young had attempted something so complicated, but not Piaget's father. Forgetting his son's young age, the father made "ironic remarks" about poor scholarship (Piaget, 1953, p. 238). When he was 8, Piaget then wrote a book entitled *Our Birds.* Rather than congratulating his son and praising such an endeavor at such a young age, his father remarked that the paper had little analysis, was "a mere compilation" (Piaget, 1953, p. 238), and was of no scholarly value. Anxious for his father's approval, Piaget wrote a book at the age of 10 about an albino sparrow that not only was published but also impressed adults so much that they thought he was an adult—and one Swiss natural science museum wanted to hire him as a curator (until they discovered how young he was). "I was 'launched,'" Piaget (1953, p. 238) remembered and that book set him working toward a research career. It might also have inadvertently made the father try writing again.

Shortly after his son's acclaim, Arthur managed to write a history of Neuchatel that was well received. It was a "ground-breaking research in local history and ... a complete renewal of Neuchatel historiography" (Vidal, 1994, p. 13) and he became more accepted by the townspeople.

The fact that Arthur Piaget was an agnostic while his wife was strongly religious was one reason, albeit a lesser one, that Piaget's parents had an unhappy marriage. In 1906, Arthur campaigned for separation of church and state. The difference in opinion with his wife on religious and personal matters made Arthur move even closer to agnostic philosophers in his study's solitary refuge. Seeking peace there amidst marital turmoil, Arthur Piaget would not allow his children to play in his study. Perhaps because he missed pleasant interaction with his father, Piaget would spend much time with his three children (two older girls and a son).

Although his own marriage was a happy one, Piaget did mimic his father in one way; with his own solitary introspection, he retreated annually to be by himself in a small cabin in the Swiss Alps for a month in the summer.

His father was also a person who had difficulty enjoying life outside of work. Arthur Piaget went to study in Paris (just like his son would later) but, despite the many attractions within the beautiful City of Lights, kept himself solely occupied with the lecture hall and library. Piaget says that he got his "love of facts" from his father, who advised his son not to study in the humanities because "it was not a true science" (Piaget, 1976, p. 7). Thus, because of his father, Piaget would turn early to the exactness of science and that would lead him to try to try to develop a theory of evolution on human learning, much like Darwin had developed for biology. Nevertheless, throughout his entire life, Piaget would refuse to write or utter unkind remarks about his father.

Observers stated, "the father and son entertain a very great affection for each other and that they are very close. Arthur Piaget, in the words of one witness, is a wonderful father, broadminded and full of understanding about his son's vocation" (Tribolet, 1996, p. 48). Neighbors commented that "Arthur Piaget exercises a great influence on his son, Jean, an influence that his…child delights in acknowledging" (Tribolet, 1996, p. 48). Indeed, in Jean Piaget's 1976 autobiography, he commented that among the many things that his father taught him was the value of systematic work, "even when he [Arthur Piaget] is carried away by the particulars" (p. 76). Vygotsky's father also valued systematic thought and work, but he was not as caustic as Piaget's father.

Vygotsky's Father

Semyon Vygodsky had "a rather stern disposition and bitter ironic humor" (Wertsch, 1985, p. 3). The persecutions and pogroms that Russian Jews suffered developed a deep bitterness within Semyon that would develop into a deep fatalism in his son. "He was a man of wide horizons, intelligent, and inclined to irony, not humor but bitter irony. The reality around him gave ample food for such an attitude" (Dobkin, 1982, p. 24). Thus, from childhood, because of persecutions and their subsequent impact on his father, Vygotsky had a predilection for literary tragedy and pathos. However, pathos is part of the germ of creativity and from this germ developed cultural–historical theory.

Semyon graduated from the Commercial Institute of Khar'kov, Ukraine. During Vygotsky's childhood, he was a department chief at the United Bank of Gomel and also an insurance salesman for a local company. After the Russian Revolution, Semyon became head of a section of the Commercial Bank of Moscow.

Semyon married a teacher in 1893 and the marriage was a happy one. His difficult personality was in sharp contrast to that of his wife, who was described as "very gentle" (Wertsch, 1985, p. 3). They were a good, complimentary contrast to each other. Semyon worked hard and earned enough income that the family was considered (like Piaget's) upper middle class. The Vygodsky family could afford a good education for their children and Semyon hired tutors for his eight children.

Semyon could also afford a large apartment in town. The spacious apartment had five large rooms and two small rooms. Three older daughters shared a large bedroom, two younger daughters shared a small bedroom, and Lev shared a bedroom with his younger brother, Dodik. This was in addition to the parents' bedroom, kitchen, dining room, and study. Unlike Arthur Piaget, Semyon's study was always open for his children's visits.

Semyon also made time for his children and did not mind interruptions to his work. When Vygotsky grew up, he allowed his children to also have open access to him. They remembered pleasant times interrupting their father. Unlike his father, Vygotsky would live in a one-room apartment that was quite cramped. From 1924 until mid-1925, that apartment was in the basement of the Psychological Institute. Then he moved to a one-room apartment at 17 Serpukhovskaya Street.

> throughout his whole life, he never had a separate room of his own. His living conditions were the least suited for scientific study. All of those colleagues and friends who would drop by would be astonished how he could concentrate on his work at the same time as there were other people in the room, someone entering, leaving, uninvolved conversations going on, children playing while he without interruption continues working. (Vygodskaya, 1994/1996, p. 1)

Vygotsky, in short, modeled his own father's behavior. Semyon and Lev could be at work, be interrupted by his children, play or listen to them, and then go immediately back to work without losing track of what they were working on. Since his father's study was often at the children's disposal, Vygotsky and his playmates "would go there to be alone for a while or to meet with a small group of friends" (Dobkin, 1982, p. 24).

Lev's parents were able to create a warm, loving climate for their children in their seven-room apartment. The Vygodsky family was among the most cultured in the city. Semyon was drawn to social activities "although any such activities were difficult to pursue at the time [because of czarist repression]. Even so, he managed to accomplish a good deal" (Dobkin, 1982, p. 24). Perhaps the strong repression suffered by Jews at the time— "the territorial restrictions, the strict quotas for entrance to the university, the prohibition from many professions, the permanent threat of the pogrom—contributed to the closeness of the family and to the prominent intellectual character of his home" (Blanck, 1990, p. 32).

Semyon believed in the need for intellectual freedom. Because Lenin began his administration by outlawing religious persecution, Semyon saw the Russian Revolution as liberating. This opinion lasted until the rise of Stalin, who Semyon saw as betraying the revolution. Lev Vygotsky would imitate his father by working to promote the Russian Revolution and, later, passively resisting Stalin's purge of intellectual freedom.

Semyon devoted evenings to his family. Many interesting conversations took place in the dining room. Every evening, it was family tradition to gather in the dining room during the obligatory evening tea at the large table. These conversations "would play a decisive role in the children's cultural formation" (Blanck, 1990, p. 32).

Conclusion

Both Piaget and Vygotsky were blessed with fathers who were free thinkers and who prodded their sons to use the ideas of Hegel and Kant. Kant's idea that one can perceive the truth through use of the will influenced both Piaget and Vygotsky to believe that they could create their respective theories. Although both fathers were stern and ironic, both genuinely loved their sons and strove to not only protect them but also to assist them in achieving greatness. Their fathers' opinion of play would also launch their son's ideas on that subject. Piaget would reject play for the child in favor of more academic pursuits. Vygotsky would not only encourage play, he would say that play precedes learning. In addition, both Piaget and Vygotsky's fathers married women who also strove to do the best that they could for their sons, despite suffering from adversity themselves.

MOTHERS

Both mothers had their positive qualities. Cecilia Vygotsky was "very gentle" (Dobkin, 1982, p. 24). Rebecca Piaget was "very intelligent, energetic, and fundamentally a very kind person" (Piaget, 1953, p. 238). Cecilia Vygotsky was a licensed teacher who devoted herself full time to her family upon marriage because women in the Victorian era were expected to drop careers upon marriage and become homemakers. In her spare time, however, Cecilia promoted cultural activities in Gomel. Rebecca Piaget initially was also a homemaker. However, by 1912, when the children were older, she decided to become active in politics. Both towns benefited from the extra work of both ladies. Both mothers also stood up for what they thought was right and this tendency became part of their sons' psyches.

Piaget's Mother

Arthur Piaget married a young, attractive Frenchwoman in Paris. "Femme tres imaginative et intelligente, elle a fait des etudes d'institutrice; tres pieuse, elle est de confession reformee [The lady is very intelligent and imaginative, a person who, by confession, very precisely reforms the study of institutions]" (Tribolet, 1996, p. 42). This tendency to speak her mind would harm her marriage and wound her children. Her bouts of anger would make Jean's home life "somewhat troublesome" (Piaget, 1953, p. 3). It also affected her childrearing. Piaget himself said, "My mother never spoiled me with too much motherly affection" (1976, p. 4). Fearing that a teacher could do what his mother did to him was one of the reasons that Piaget would require a passive role for the teacher.

When her three children reached elementary school age, Rebecca entered politics and started working with the Swiss Red Cross. Because Rebecca Piaget had strong convictions and did not mind speaking them, both of these endeavors got her into trouble. Piaget's mother became the first woman socialist elected to the local school commission. During World War I, she supported a minister for reelection who had been imprisoned as a conscientious objector. She also became involved in the maintenance of humane treatment of prisoners of war. She included her son on trips to hospitals and POW camps. These visits strengthened Piaget's already ingrained concern for humanity.

Rebecca Piaget was French and she sided with the Allies during the war. In 1914, she published in a local newspaper her impressions of the conditions in refugee camps on the French side of Lake Geneva. Her charges about German Red Cross nurses poisoning Allied soldiers antagonized the president of the German Red Cross. He brought legal action against her for libel. After her trial and a series of appeals, she was found guilty of reporting a slandering rumor but was acquitted because she did not defame anybody in particular.

Rebecca caused her son's first hospitalization for a nervous breakdown when she insisted, against her husband's objections, that Jean Piaget take confirmation lessons when he was 15. During the 6 weeks' course on fundamentals of Christian doctrine, Piaget came to see the difficulty of reconciling science and religion. In particular, he had problems with the "fragility" (Piaget, 1953, p. 239) of the five proofs for the existence of God that he was taught in his confirmation class.

Jean Piaget was caught in a tug of war between two parents of strong will. "My father, on the other hand, did not attend church, and I quickly sensed that for him the current faith and an honest historical criticism were incompatible" (Piaget, 1953, p. 239). Later, Piaget found a book by Auguste Sabatier in his father's study, entitled *La philosohie de la religion fondee sur la psychologie et l'historie,* and this caused a second crisis.

Another reason that Piaget's first mental hospitalization occurred was he could not reconcile God to the carnage that the world was enduring with World War I. The second crisis came when he could not reconcile the logic of science with the faith of theology. To help, his godfather and uncle, Samuel Cornut, invited him to spend some quiet time at Lake Annecy. There, Cornut introduced Jean Piaget to the "creative evolution" of Henri Bergson. Bergson's considered evolution of moral concepts was crucial to Piaget's intellectual development. Bergson rejected Darwinism, which Piaget did not do, and added moral reasons for the evolution of philosophical and biological ideas. This would later allow Bergson to provide for evolutionary ethics with scientific foundations. It was just the next step for Piaget to go from reading about biological evolution to reading about philosphical evolution to wanting to create an epistemology that traced the evolution of human learning.

At first, however, this clash between philosophy and science was too much for Piaget. "The shock was terrific" (Piaget, 1953, p. 240) and Piaget entered a sanitarium at Leysin. A child can react just as much against a parent's influence as in favor of it. The result of his parent's actions may have triggered two hospitalizations but they also resulted in two important resolves; namely, Piaget would reject organized religion in favor of philosophy and he would try to use science to purge philosophy of its irrational nature. Children of a mentally unstable parent fear sometimes that they might go insane. Piaget worried about the conflict within him that now took place between his speculative and scientific sides. This mental tug of war represented the origins of Piaget's lifelong preoccupation with how scientific methods are enlisted in the service of imagination. Piaget had to clear his thinking of any irrational nature. This included psychoanalysis.

It was Rebecca who influenced her son to reject psychoanalysis and the work of Sigmund Freud. Zurich was the Protestant capital of psychoanalysis and Piaget became interested in it during his spring seminar at the University of Zurich—probably also because of his own two nervous breakdowns and in an attempt to find a cure for his mother and prevent further breakdowns of himself. Later, when in Paris as a young man, Piaget further investigated Freud's work and even allowed himself (Piaget) to be psychoanalyzed several times. During one of the sessions, he remembered being kidnapped as a child at age 8. The memory was very real to him (Piaget, 1966a). Mentioning this to his mother, she assured him that it never happened. Taken aback by how real this memory of a fictitious event was, Piaget then rejected psychoanalysis.

Piaget reported that he felt a "silent hostility" toward his mother that "has existed for a long time" (1920, p. 21). Piaget attributed his two nervous breakdowns to "family conditions and to the intellectual curiosity characteristic of that productive age" (1953, p. 239). Piaget's mother was eventually hospitalized by her husband for 3 months at Dr. Henri Bersot's clinic in Le Landeron, Switzerland (Piaget, 1927).

> Her rather neurotic temperament, however, made our family life somewhat troublesome. One of the direct consequences of this situation was that I started to forego playing for serious work very early; this I obviously did as much to imitate my father as to take refuge in both a private and a non-fictitious world. Indeed, I have always detested any departure from reality, an attitude which I relate to the second important influential factor of my early life [the first one was his father] viz., my mother's poor mental health; it was this disturbing factor which, at the beginning of my studies in psychology, made me intensely interested in questions of psychoanalysis and pathological psychology [, which Piaget would study in Paris]. Though this interest helped me to achieve independence and to widen my cultural background, I have never since felt any desire to involve myself deeper in that particular direction, always much preferring the study of normalcy and of the workings of the intellect to that of the tricks of the unconscious. (Piaget, 1953, p. 238)

Vygotsky's Mother

Little is known about Cecilia Vygodskaya. Except for information from Semyon Dobkin, her son's boyhood friend, no primary information exists on her. Dobkin (1982) writes that people who knew her remembered that she was kind and gentle. The fact that she renounced her teaching career to raise a family speaks to her sense of self-sacrifice. She knew German well and often read the poet Heine's works to her family in the evenings. Writing in 19th-century German, Heine's poems mix beauty with irony in a way that gives them a cynical tone. Such poetry would fit her husband's personality and the difficulties of living in a country prone to hurt those of her faith.

Cecilia also introduced her children to the philosophy of Spinoza. Spinoza was a 17th-century Dutch Jew who wrote that mankind's highest happiness consists in coming to understand and appreciate the truth. Spinoza was denounced by some Jews because of his all-inclusive, pantheistic view of the nature of God. He wrote that God has many attributes but mankind can only know two of them: mind and matter. Vygotsky would be influenced by Heine and Spinoza.

The closeness and warmth of family gatherings was of her making. She also prodded her husband to take a more active role in the welfare of Gomel. Together, they not only founded and paid for the local library, but they also helped start local theatrical productions. Vygotsky received his love of literature from his mother, who would often read literature out loud to the family during the long winter nights. These readings of Shakespeare, Tolstoy, Goethe, Pushkin, and other authors influenced Vygotsky to see language as a tool of learning (Rissom, 1985).

Because Cecilia also taught grammar and literature while a teacher, she was able to pass this love of language on to her offspring. For example, her third child, Zinaida, would become a noted linguist and philologist. Together, this mother and his sister planted a seed in Vygotsky's mind that language was a tool of learning. In the Victorian Era, women were expected to achieve through their sons. Her searches "would become her son's searches; namely, adventures of the spirit" (Levitin, 1982).

Conclusion

Their relationship with their mothers resulted in both Piaget and Vygotsky wanting to contribute to the common good. Because of his mother's humanitarian actions, Piaget would be a humanitarian himself trying to reform learning. Because of his mother's cultural and educational endeavors, Vygotsky would create cultural–historical theory to improve education.

Both mothers loved their children. However, Cecilia had to deal with a dysfunctional society that would eventually kill two of her sons: Dodik and Lev. Rebecca had to deal with a dysfunctional mind. No one asks for persecution and no one asks for mental instability. It just happens. Both sets of mothers and sons struggled together to deal with their difficult situations. Both sons became stronger men because of their mothers' presence in this struggle, but both men developed a different role for the teacher because of their mothers. Piaget's would be passive and Vygotsky's would be active.

SIBLINGS

There is a distinct difference between Piaget and Vygotsky when it comes to sibling relationships. Piaget had two younger sisters but there is no record of him being very close to them. On the other hand, Vygotsky was very close to his seven siblings and cousins. For Vygotsky, this relationship would endorse the social aspects of learning. For Piaget, this lonely relationship would confirm the advantage of solitary inquiry.

Piaget's Siblings

Piaget was photographed in his childhood with his two sisters, Madelaine and Marthe. However, there is no record of him ever being close to them. Of course, there were probably family celebrations and outings, but the only written connection between Piaget and his sisters dealt with hospitalizations. Piaget's youngest sister, Marthe, was hospitalized once for mental nervousness. Piaget's father had people believe that it was for his children's physical health that they went to the mountain health resort of Leysin, which also had hotels that functioned as tuberculosis sanitariums. People with nervous disorders also went there for rest. Tuberculosis was a more respectable disease than a mental breakdown (Vidal, 1989).

Vygotsky's Siblings

Vygotsky was close to all members of his family. Among his siblings, however, he was especially close to his sister, Zinaida, and his brother, Dodik.

Zinaida was a remarkable person. She loved literature and language. Often, she was part of the playgroups in the neighborhood that put on theatrical productions or held literary discussions and debates. Zinaida was an excellent student whose academic achievements appeared to be curtailed by Russian social rules. Women were not allowed to enter the Imperial Moscow University. However, in 1915, Zinaida won a berth at the Non Credit Women's University Courses in Moscow. There, she shared a room with Lev for 2 years. She also kept herself informed of his interests. Perhaps because of her mother's influence, she chose the philosophy of Spinoza as the theme of her dissertation. The Russian Revolution opened up avenues for women that had been closed to them earlier. Thus, upon graduation, Zinaida became coauthor of many foreign language dictionaries and a prominent linguist. "Constant contact with her must have influenced the scientific interests of Vygotsky" (Dobkin, 1982, p. 33).

Although 3 years younger, Dodik was very close to Vygotsky. Together with their cousin, David, their neighborhood friends, Semyon Dobkin, and his sister, Fanya, they started a Jewish history study circle over which Zinaida presided. This activity lasted for 2 years and eventually led to the study of the philosophy of history. In addition, Dodik was part of all the dramas, debates, and literary discussions that Vygotsky held in his youth. Indeed, Dodik, Dobkin, and Vygotsky were so close that they were called the "Gomel troika"

(Dobkin, 1982, p. 34). Vygotsky became such a leader of their cultural activities at home and their intellectual discussions at school that, by 1911, he was dubbed "the little professor" (Dobkin, 1982, p. 34).

Of promising scholarship, Dodik never lived to achieve the intellectual levels of his older brother. The Russian Revolution took place during World War I. The combined conflicts resulted in severe shortages of fuel and food. With such deprivations, Dodik contracted tuberculosis. Because Gomel expected an enemy attack, doctors suggested the family take Dodik to the Crimea for rest and recuperation. The warmer climate, they thought, had healing properties. Both Lev and his mother decided to make the journey. Unfortunately, they became trapped in Kiev between the Red and White armies and never made it to the Crimea.

Dodik died in Kiev. He was only 12 years old. His death crushed his mother and older brother. Vygotsky's already dark fatalism deepened. He looked around for solace. Vygotsky discovered many intellectuals in Kiev were then doing jobs for which they had not been trained. Kiev seemed to be the "hotbed" (Daniels, 1993, p. 205) into which many intellectual elite had been thrown to start anew. It was while he was in Kiev that Vygotsky changed his profession to education.

"It was an era of new projects, new beginnings, and young enthusiasts seemed to be in every office of Kiev, working on projects for a paradise on earth" (Ehrenburg, 1962, p. 291). Depressed by his brother's death and willing to make a contribution toward remaking his country, Vygotsky decided to change fields. Prior to the Revolution, Jews could not be public school teachers. Lenin opened up the profession to them. When Vygotsky returned with his mother to Gomel, he became a public high school teacher.

Conclusion

While Piaget's relationship with his sisters cemented his idea about the solitary independence of the learner, Vygotsky's relationship with his siblings cemented the idea that learning is a social experience and that knowledge can be given by a "social other." These ideas were further developed during their elementary education.

ELEMENTARY EDUCATION

While formal education failed Piaget but benefited Vygotsky, informal education benefited both youngsters. In the case of Piaget, it was only outside the classroom (with mentors that were not designated at the time by society to be his "social other") that he succeeded. His mentors succeeded by the method they used. First, they prescribed an academic challenge that was just a bit higher than his chronological age. Then, they set the environment so that he could meet that challenge. This method would eventually become part of Piaget's pedagogy because, from this, Piaget would form the idea of the "optimal mismatch." Vygotsky, on the other hand, never lacked for excellent classroom instruction by those whom society set to be his "social other," namely, parents, siblings, and teachers. Because of such excellent formal education, Vygotsky would define a role for a "social other" that was very active.

Piaget

In 1907, Piaget entered the Latin School. There, both his grades and his oral examinations were very high and he graduated with the highest marks. However, the teachers who had the greatest influence on him were not his classroom teachers, but those who encouraged his independent and solitary pursuit of his intellectual interests outside of school. In his autobiography, Piaget recalled that in his little elementary school class, no teacher encouraged students to spend time in pursuit of knowledge of their own choosing. Piaget recalled that "There were three kinds of boys in his class: lazy, conscientious, and those [like himself] who were only moderately good pupils in school, but who went for more interesting things at home...anything you like except what was on the curriculum" (Piaget, 1953, p. 352).

The educational lesson for Piaget from his elementary school was that "the conscientious boys became civil servants...and the lazy did not do worse" (Piaget, 1953, p. 353). Piaget remembers that he and his classmates were always being told that, if they "would only spend on their homework a quarter of the time you spend on your personal pursuits, you would do exceedingly well" (p. 352). The result was that Piaget only wished that he had spent even more time on interests of his own choosing—instead of those chosen for him by his teachers.

Thus, early in the formation of his pedagogical theory, Piaget would form the concept of a teacher as a diagnostician who would create a classroom environment set to the children's chronological stage of development and allow the children to engage in independent, intellectual classroom pursuits.

Piaget started his own informal education quite early in life. "From seven to ten years of age, I became successively interested in mechanics, in birds, in fossils of secondary and tertiary layers, and in seashells," remembered Piaget (Evans, 1981, p. 107). Being unhappy both at home and in school caused the young Piaget to turn to a mentor.

Functioning as a surrogate uncle, Paul Godet was head of the local museum of natural sciences. He employed Jean Piaget, starting when Piaget was a 10-year-old, to classify mollusks and snails. This "job" was the most valuable part of the youngster's informal early education. Piaget always remembered his days with Godet as happy and very educational—much more so than his Latin School classroom instruction. The youngster's pay was some free specimens at the end of the year. Under the guidance of Godet, Piaget became interested in the classification of animals and how they can learn at chronological stages. He also became interested in classifying the evolution of mollusks but had to leave that pursuit when he attended the university. Later, upon returning to Switzerland after a stint in Paris, he would continue this work.

Vygotsky

Vygotsky received his primary education at home with a private but remarkable tutor, Solomon Ashpiz, who taught Vygotsky the value of inquiry in lessons. Ashpiz had been exiled to Siberia for taking part in a revolutionary movement. He found his way to Gomel and, there, made a living by tutoring. He was a mathematician by training but taught all the other subjects as well. Ashpiz was described as "a wonderfully gentle person. A kind, good-humored man" (Dobkin, 1982, p. 25). He taught his students by the Socratic method. "Ashpiz's pedagogical technique was apparently grounded in a form of ingenious Socratic dialogue, which left his students, especially one as gifted as Lev Semenovich [Vygotsky], with well-developed, inquisitive minds" (Wertsch, 1985, p. 4).

Ashpiz would teach his students by asking a question. As they were answering it, he would close his eyes. Although it appeared that he was asleep, actually he was not. He would not interrupt while the student was answering. However, when the child finished, he would open his eyes and would ask the student to repeat the places that were wrong. It immediately became clear that he had not missed a single word, and it immediately became clear to the student where the error lay. "His pupils benefited a great deal from the fact that he made them think independently" (Dobkin, 1982, p. 25). Vygotsky learned so well under Ashpiz that he did not enter the first 4 years at the local gymnasium, which taught students for the last 6 years before either their formal education ended or they went on to university level. When Vygotsky did enter the gymnasium (similar to an American high school), he was so well educated by Ashpiz that he was able to become the top scholar of the school and graduate in 2 years. Because all those put in the role of the "social other" were nurturing and helpful,

Vygotsky would make the teacher's role in the classroom active and have sharing of learning among those in the classroom.

Vygotsky also had a fine informal education. He set up his own debating societies, literary discussion groups, and theatricals. While Gomel had no formal organizations for its youth, outside of religious activities, the Vygodsky family saw to it that a great deal of learning took place in a cultural environment. (This will be further discussed later.)

Conclusion

In conclusion, the formal education of Piaget stifled rather than encouraged his genius. In the case of Vygotsky, however, his formal education helped him. Piaget would remember the instruction at the Latin School negatively when he wrote his pedagogy—even though he graduated with the highest marks. Likewise, Vygotsky would remember his tutor when he devised a more active role for the teacher. It was also during these early years that Piaget discovered error was not bad. You can learn as much from your laboratory mistakes as you can from your successes. However, it was also during those early years that Vygotsky developed the idea error is to be avoided, because error could get you killed or hurt in 20th-century Russia.

It was working with specimens at the Neuchatel Museum of Natural Science that created the ideal of equilibration for Piaget. He observed how these animals adapted to their environment. When coupled with introspection about how he himself learned his subjects, Piaget came up with the idea that one first observes a problem, internalizes it in one's mind and thereby creating a solution, and then performing the solution. Vygotsky came up with the same idea but, instead of calling it equilibration, he called it internalization by observing how he and others learned and created in their Gomel "play" groups and tutoring. These ideas, forming in their childhood, developed further during their adolescence. Those years had great difficulties.

CHAPTER 2

ADOLESCENCE

INTRODUCTION

The change from children to teenagers brought both men into circumstances that solidified the basic ideas of their learning theories. The two most noticeable aspects of Piaget's self-created character were an obsession with developing a rational epistemology and a spirit of perpetual but individualized inquiry. The two most noticeable aspects of Vygotsky's self-created character were a drive to demonstrate that learning was a social–historical vehicle and the belief that language was the tool that drove that vehicle. Both graduated from their secondary schools in 1912. Both were influenced by the same philosophers and read them while teenagers. Both became known as local authorities in their fields at the same time—biology for Piaget and literary analysis for Vygotsky.

FRIENDS

The influences of friends were very different for both men. Vygotsky had many "social others" in the form of close family, good friends, and effective teachers who also functioned as effective mentors. So, Vygotsky would develop the idea that learning takes place via a "social other." Piaget had a dysfunctional family, no really close friends, and all his teachers did him more harm than good (Piaget, 1952). So, Piaget would write of the independence of the learner. Remembering the hurts that took place during

---

Parallel Paths to Constructivism: Jean Piaget and Lev Vygotsky, pages 21–35
Copyright © 2004 by Information Age Publishing
21

his childhood, Piaget would insist that the teacher be only a diagnostician who would correctly create an academically rich classroom environment set at the student's chronological age of development, with just a bit of an optimal mismatch or intellectual challenge to entice the student to strive toward the top of his stage of development.

Piaget

While liked by his peers and a member of their clubs, Piaget's closest companions were adults that served as his mentors. The intertwining of people, institutions, and ideas in Piaget's youth produced a Christian, social network that exposed a range of possibilities and shaped early choices. These set a direction for his later development.

While attending three local clubs and the gymnasium, Piaget would later increase his circle of friends; however, they were always older, in the form of mentors, and functioned as diagnosticians (a role that Piaget would later give to the teacher). Their role and names are described more fully in the section, "Clubs and Hobbies." In contrast, Vygotsky had many close childhood friends. In addition, his parents and siblings also shared friendship with Vygotsky. Thus, Vygotsky called for a "social other" that would scaffold a child up to the top of the ZPD, because this is what happened with the friends that Vygotsky had.

Vygotsky

Besides his own brother and sister, Vygotsky also bonded with children in the neighborhood. Two of these were his cousin, David, and a neighbor, Semyon Dobkin.

Lev's cousin, David, whose family spelled their name Vygodsky, was several years older than Lev and had "great influence over him" (Blanck, 1990, p. 35). David helped direct the "play" in the neighborhood. Because of him, many literary discussions as well as debates and dramas were performed. David became interested in Esperanto. Writing in that international language meant that one could correspond all over the world. David not only did so, he got the other two members of his "troika" (Lev and Semyon Dobkin) to do so as well. David also knew several foreign languages. He encouraged Lev Vygotsky to learn Hebrew, German, French, Latin, Greek, and English. The three had pen pals and Lev's lived in Iceland.

David was bright and entered St. Petersburg University. There, he studied philology. Lev would also later major in this subject. David later studied at the University of Petrograd where he joined a group of young linguists who came up with the theory of reforming literature by studying the play of language forms. Since language always interested Vygotsky, David shared this idea with him. Vygotsky would remember this when he made language the tool of learning.

David became a competent poet, although by profession he was a linguist and philologist. He became noted for translating Russian poetry into Spanish and Hebrew literature into Russian (van der Veer & Valsiner, 1991). He familiarized Lev with the works of many noted linguists: Roman Jakobson, Viktor Shklovsky, and Lev Jakubinsky. These famous members of the Formalist school became common references in Vygotsky's work (Blanck, 1990). David returned to Gomel in 1919. Like Vygotsky, he taught literature at the local public school. Like Vygotsky, in his spare time, he became a publisher.

Together with Semyon Dobkin and Lev Vygotsky, David started a publishing venture called "Ages of Days." Its goal was to print inexpensive editions of good literary works. However, due to paper shortages in the USSR after the revolution, some commissars closed down their enterprise after only two publications in 1920. David then left for St. Petersburg, where he obtained employment. Unfortunately, he kept up his Esperanto correspondence. Esperanto became a suspected activity during Stalin's reign because, in an attempt to create a world language, it involved communication outside of the USSR.

David also became involved in the Spanish Civil War, where he served as an intermediary between Soviet and anti-Franco authorities. The USSR backed the royalist cause in that revolution and looked for scapegoats when Franco won. David was arrested on a charge of espionage in 1938, convicted of anti-Soviet activity, and sentenced to a gulag. Efforts by the writer Marietta Shaginjan and David's other literary friends "to get him released failed" (Shaginjan in Meldvedev, 1974, p. 806). He died in a concentration camp in mid-1942.

Semyon Dobkin was 3 years older than Lev Vygotsky. Nevertheless, they were friends "from childhood" (Dobkin, 1982, p. 23). Dobkin wrote the first biography of Lev and was the only member of the "Gomel troika" to live into old age. He died a natural death in the late 1980s. Dobkin remembered, "We were never friends in the every-day sense. Our relations were based on our mutual interests in questions which we thought were crucial for understanding life" (Dobkin, 1982, p. 24).

Most of the knowledge about Vygotsky's youth comes from Dobkin's biography of him. Dobkin remembers being part of "play" circles that really were learning experiences. Vygotsky set up cultural and learning activities with Dobkin's sister, Fanya, his own sister, Zinaida, and David. One of the first was a study group on Jewish history. Concerned with the persecutions against them, Zinaida decided to form this with Fanya and some girls from the fourth form at the local elementary school. They decided to let the boys in and Vygotsky quickly became a leader. The group quickly departed from the pragmatic study of history to discover the philosophy of history. Dobkin remembers that Vygotsky was very enthusiastic about Hegel's view of history with its dialectical formula of thesis, antithesis, and synthesis. Vygotsky applied this idea to their studies of historical events.

> Many people know Vygotsky principally as a general psychologist and a researcher in the study of the handicapped and a student of art. Actually he was first and foremost a thinker in the fullest sense of the word. He was a historical thinker. His historical approach to any problem, characteristic of all his scientific work, took shape in those early years. (Dobkin, 1982, p. 16)

History is sometimes played out as a game of chess. It was Dobkin who got David and Lev involved in stamp collecting and playing chess. Dobkin wrote that an example of Vygotsky's thinking could be found in his chess games. "Vygotsky was a good player...but he was fond of non-standard gambits" (Dobkin, 1982, p. 27). That is because Vygotsky could see both sides of an issue at the same time. The Gomel group often held literary discussions. Dobkin remembers Vygotsky giving him Alexander Potebnya's book, *Thought and Language*. Although it was primarily a study in linguistics, it did contain some psychology. Dobkin believed that this book provided a starting point for Vygotsky's own *Thought and Speech.*

Later, while at the university, Vygotsky read William James's work, *The Varieties of Religious Experience*. It was also a psychological work investigating mystical experiences. On vacation back in Gomel, Vygotsky gave it to Dobkin because it seemed so impressive. During the discussion session, Dobkin became aware that Vygotsky had an ability to look at all sides of an issue. "I think his replies revealed a characteristic trait of his thinking, namely the ability to see a problem from different, often opposite angles, the desire not to miss an important phenomenon only because it appears to be incredible" (1982, p. 34).

Dobkin also remembered that Vygotsky read a second book in psychology during this time. It was Sigmund *Freud's Zur Pschopatologie des Alltagslebens [Through Psychopathology to Old Age]*. "Freud's ideas were new and unusual for us, and they provoked thought about the underlying causes of many psychic phenomena" (Dobkin, 1982, p. 34). Although psychology was part of Vygotsky's curriculum at the History and Philosophy Department at Shanyavsky University, Dobkin believed that the two books they reviewed in 1917 "were a great stimulus to Vygotsky's interest in psychology" (1982, p. 34).

Semyon Dobkin became a schoolteacher of history at the Dnieper Naval Flotilla. "While my work at school was interesting, I felt that it was not challenging enough" (1982, p. 34). Later, Lev would also become a schoolteacher. Dobkin had read a Russian translation of the novel *Richard Ferlong* in *Russkaya Mysl* magazine. It was about an engraver who publishes books, printing them himself. "All this appealed to me very much, so I [Vygotsky] decided that…I would go into publishing" (Dobkin, 1982, p. 35). He confined his plans to Vygotsky who decided to put those plans into action and include David Vygodsky. The result was their "Ages of Days" publishing firm that lasted for about a year. When it was closed down because Russian authorities were confiscating paper to ease the Kremlin's paper shortage, Semyon went to Moscow for further study. Vygotsky remained in Gomel teaching school until 1924.

> I had an opportunity to visit Gomel for a few days [in 1921] to see my friends and relations. I met Vygotsky there. Only a year had passed since we parted, but he was in a totally different company, surrounded by young people unknown to me including, I think, students from the Teachers' College. Again, he was not in very good health, but he tried to keep going. There were few people of kindred spirit left in Gomel, both his sisters and David Vygodsky having left town, but Vygotsky did not want to leave his parents. (Dobkin, 1982, p. 37)

At that time, Vygotsky was apolitical and had not yet decided whether or not to become a Soviet (Blanck, 1990). Although his daughter, Gita, recalled that he "was always a Soviet" (G. Vygodskaya, personal communication, October 21, 1988), Vygotsky needed some time at home to make that decision.

In 1925, Dobkin heard about Vygotsky's appointment to the Experimental Psychological Institute in Moscow. This building also housed Moscow University's departments of history and philology. Dobkin had classes in that building but they did not get a chance to meet. Dobkin was a busy student of philosophy at the University of Moscow and Vygotsky was very busy at the Institute. They lost touch with each other for 4 years. Moscow was a far larger city than Gomel and, with the longer distances and the pressures of daily life, they did not see each other as often as before. "Besides, he had became immersed in psychology while I had chosen a different occupation, publishing" (Dobkin, 1982, p. 37).

When the two friends next met, Dobkin was saddened by his friend's failing health. Vygotsky had moved away from general investigations in psychology to developmental psychology. "He was a pioneer in various fields of special psychology in the Soviet Union. That work increasingly carried him away. Neither illness nor any other circumstances could tear him away from that important and engrossing work" (Dobkin, 1982, p. 38). Dobkin remembered visiting Vygotsky just before he died. Vygotsky told Dobkin that he wanted Dobkin to go with him to Sukhumi. Vygotsky had a job offer there but did not want to go alone. Although he had other commitments, Dobkin agreed but those plans never materialized. Vygotsky's health rapidly grew worse. He died at the Serebryany Bor Sanatorium of tuberculosis in 1934. His last words were, "I'm ready" (Dobkin, 1982, p. 38).

Conclusion

The qualities of their childhood friendships had much to do with Piaget's and Vygotsky's later theories. Piaget's friends were not as close to him as Vygotsky's. They only influenced genetic epistemology in that they proved the independence of the learner; namely, that one can have a productive learning experience without contact from others. However, for Vygotsky, friends were all important. They proved time after time how learning is a social experience. This was also proven to Vygotsky through clubs and hobbies.

CLUBS AND HOBBIES

Clubs and hobbies were very important toward the development of Vygotsky's and Piaget's ideas. What Piaget lacked in close personal relationships with his siblings and peers, he made up for with relationships in three local clubs that widened the door for closer relationships with older mentors. Vygotsky's close relationships with people that society had placed in the relationship of the "social other" were cemented with informal clubs and hobbies. In the case of both men, their clubs and hobbies honed their thinking, oratorical, and writing skills.

Piaget

Besides being a seat of canton government and the local university, Neuchatel offered various and well-organized clubs and private societies aimed at fostering knowledge through independent research. Piaget quickly renounced play for more productive inquiry. It was within this community's framework (where everybody knew everybody) that learning was respected and openly shared. According to a local writer and literary critic, some of the buildings constructed in town, like the university and museum where Piaget volunteered from age 10 until entering the local university "bore witness to the city's intellectual effort toward justifying better renown as a school town" (Godet, 1901, p. 52).

Prominent among Neuchatel's learned societies and amateur clubs were the Jura Club, Friends of Nature, and Swiss Christian Students' Association. Piaget belonged to all three and any friendships that he had with his peers were because of those organizations. Again, those who helped him most were older mentors, who by happy circumstances happened to belong to those clubs.

Paul Godet, Piaget's earliest childhood mentor and curator of the Neuchatel Museum of Natural History, was a member of the Jura Club that encouraged local studies of natural history. Godet and Pierre Bovet were honorary members of the Friends of Nature. Bovet was a militant Protestant that would become a mentor for Piaget when Piaget joined the Swiss Christian Students' Association. He also directed the Jean-Jacques Rousseau Institute until 1933. His cousin, Edouard Claparede, who would become a minor mentor and then boss of Piaget, would establish that institute and both men would invite Piaget to join them in 1925, thus launching Piaget's career.

Both the Jura and Friends of Nature were dedicated to the individual study of local fauna and flora. This channeled Piaget's adolescent energy into what Piaget thought were healthy and morally acceptable directions. Both clubs functioned exactly the way that Piaget would later structure his Piaget Institute. Members would meet, discuss courses of study, and, then, each individual member would be off in natural science pursuits of individual interest. Piaget also joined the Christian Students' Association, for which Bovet was secretary. Both became contributors to the organization's social and religious journal. Thus, all three of these formal clubs served as Vygotsky's more informal clubs were to serve; that is, they channeled Piaget's thinking and provided a vehicle to improve oratorical and writing skills.

The Jura Club was founded in 1865 at the initiative of the local doctor Louis Guillaume (Vidal, 1994). It was the naturalist's counterpart of the local historical society. Its goal was to acquaint Neuchatel's young people with the local fauna and flora by involving them in interesting field trips to collect specimens. They also had lectures by local professors on the natural specimens and local biological history of the area. In short, the Jura Club was "a model of intelligent pedagogy, capable of promoting work in common and self-esteem, as well as morality and personal responsibility" (Buisson, 1882, p. 3).

The Friends of Nature grew out of the Natural Sciences Society of Neuchatel, which was founded in 1832. In May 1893, a junior adjunct club was formed from this adult group. Pierre Bovet co-founded it with a friend, Carl Albert Loosli. Since he was Piaget's mentor, it was natural for Bovet to ask Piaget to become a member. Membership was restricted to those 14 years of age and above who would "apply themselves to the natural sciences" (Bovet, 1943, p. 1) with a goal to instructing each other in the various branches. Godet was granted honorary membership. Direct observation was the essence of the club's activities and, interestingly enough, that would be the essence of the role for Piaget's teachers. The club organized field trips, published interesting projects in a local journal, and held periodic readings of interesting research. Piaget participated in all of these activities.

Finally, the Swiss Christian Students' Association (ACSE) contributed to Piaget's identity as a young Christian intellectual (Vidal, 1994). It also led to cementing his mother's wish for him to become a Christian socialist. It was one of the reasons that he wrote the essay, *The Mission of the Idea*. The ACSE belonged to the Universal Federation of Christian Students' Associations, established in 1895 by the American John Mott (Vidal, 1994). Its goal was to "bring together all those who sincerely search and help them approach the person of Christ as a living personality and not as an object of theological argument" (Buscarlet, 1920, p. 8). In a book, *Reschere,* Piaget portrayed this club as a "fertile movement" (Piaget, 1918/1980, p. 38). "It had no creed and no political line and...wished to reconcile everything" (Vidal, 1994, p. 106). Its conception of what its young members should know closely merged with the new scientific and literary discourses of the time (Vidal, 1994). This club believed that there was a link between religion and youth. Youth were to regenerate Christianity and, especially after the horrors of World War I, were to strive to bring a better, godly way to the world (Vidal, 1994).

I believe that the clubs in which Piaget had an active membership were directly responsible for the growth of his ideas. They gave him new methods of inquiry, created at least one crisis that changed his life, provided him with mentors, and gave him a mission by which he could improve the world; namely, creating a rational method of instruction. Vidal writes that the clubs Piaget joined, and his mentors, show the "cohesion of the social context in which he grew up" (Vidal, 1994, p. 21).

So, Piaget grew up with the help of older diagnosticians who were able to compensate for his solitary life. These clubs led Piaget toward "the original problem motivating...his work; namely, an attempt to reconcile science and values" (Chapman, 1988, Preface). Piaget's clubs also encouraged him in his hobby of writing and encouraged the shy lad to speak in public. For example, the ACSE's journal published Piaget's *The Mission of the Idea* and the Friends of Nature encouraged him to give lectures. Thus, Piaget's formal clubs were as supportive as Vygotsky's informal ones.

Vygotsky

Vygotsky did not belong to any formally organized clubs. However, as already mentioned, he did form and was a leader of many informal organizations. He also, as already mentioned, had several hobbies. The "playgroups," hobbies, and informal clubs that Vygotsky organized were really learning experiences.

> The play–development relationship can be compared to the instruction–development relationship, play provides a much wider background for changes in needs and consciousness. Action in the imaginative sphere, in an imaginary situation, the creation of voluntary intentions, and the formation of real-life plans and volitional motives—all appear in play and make it the highest level of preschool development. (1978, pp. 102–103)

As stated, Vygotsky's mother, sister, cousins, and playgroups encouraged him to read and analyze the written word so it was not that large of a jump for Vygotsky to write literary analysis. In 1912, Vygotsky also wrote an analysis of Bunin's poetry, including Bruin's *Light Breathing*. He included this analysis in his dissertation, *The Psychology of Art*. Finally, Vygotsky wrote an essay on Krylov's fables that was included in a slightly modified form in his dissertation.

"Literature, especially his favorite poetry, always gave him much solace in life and always engaged his attention" (Dobkin, in Wertsch, 1985, p. 20). "Like all Russian school children, he knew a great deal of Pushkin's poetry" (Wertsch, 1985, p. 4) but, unlike most children, preferred the tragic, pathos passages. The tragic poems of Blok also attracted him. When he went to Moscow, the works of Dostoyevsky moved him. He saw them performed at the Moscow Art Theater and became particularly attracted to *The Brothers Karamazov* and *The Possessed*. During his student years, Vygotsky became interested in the poetry of the satirical poet Sasha Cherny. He also grew even more fond of Tyutchev's poetry and those of Blok. "These poems tell us something of Vygotsky's perception of the world at the time" (Dobkin, 1982, p. 32). "His literary interests are more revealing than his early scientific interests" (Dobkin, 1982, p. 32).

Dobkin believed that Vygotsky's interest in fiction led to his interest in psychology. "In part, the turn to that science was a natural corollary of his interest in fiction, notably the psychological novel. At the same time, his acquaintance with some scholarly works quickened his interest in the subject" (Dobkin, 1982, p. 33). Two such works were Alexander Potebnya's *Thought and Language* and William James's *The Varieties of Religious Experience*. Vygotsky read these in 1917.

Vygotsky always had a great love for the theater (Dobkin, 1982). "For the milieu in which Vygotsky lived, the Art Theater taught them something about the outside world, and its productions provoked thoughts about life and oneself. His interest in theater led to his acquaintance with the then famous theater critics, Nikolai and Abram Efros" (Dobkin, 1982, p. 34). Vygotsky staged Gogol's play, "The Marriage," during a summer vacation while still a schoolboy (Dobkin, 1982). He also never missed a single play at the Gomel theater. Vygotsky's "play" group put on dramas in his youth.

After the university, Vygotsky headed the theater section of the Gomel Department of People's Education or Narodnoe Obrazovanie. One of its organizers was Ivan Danjushevsky, who later invited Vygotsky to work in Moscow in the field of defectology when Danjushevsky was tapped to head up a newly created department in the Ministry of Education for postwar handicapped children (Prawat, 2002). Vygotsky took an active part in the selection of the repertoire, the choice of sets, and he also helped direct it. In addition, he edited the theater section of the local newspaper, *Polesskaja Pravada* (van der Veer & Valsiner, 1991). This interest would lead to a paper on the psychology of the actor, which he wrote in 1933 (Vygotsky, 1937).

Once enrolled in the University at Moscow, Vygotsky's law studies had an impact on his cultural activities in Gomel. Dobkin remembered during the summers of 1915 and 1916 that Vygotsky would set up a literary court with his Gomel friends and a newcomer, Vladimir Uzin. One of their cases was Garshin's *Natalia Nikolayevna*.

> It was about a man who commits murder out of jealousy. Vygotsky did not mind being either the prosecutor or defense counsel. Then I realized that he could see the arguments in favor of both sides. He had acquired this approach to analyzing cases as a law student. But his whole mode of thinking was such as to defy one-sideness, prejudice and undue confidence in the correctness of a particular conception. His whole scientific career was marked by his extraordinary ability to understand not only the things with which he himself could identify but also the other's point of view. (Dobkin, 1982, p. 30)

The conclusion is, then, that Vygotsky was an active and prominent member of the cultural life wherever he lived and his friends were enlisted in this promotion of culture. His diverse activities in this field led to his meeting prominent authors. For example, the poet Nadezhda Mandel'shtam dedicated his 1922 work to Vygotsky (Mandel'shtam, 1920). She recalls that Vygotsky was "a man of great intellect" (Mandel'shtam, 1970, p. 241).

Conclusion

The clubs and hobbies that both Piaget and Vygotsky enjoyed as children also opened the door to meeting new people who assisted them in formulating their respective learning theories. In addition, their recreational activities (whether formalized, like Piaget's, or organized on an informal basis, like Vygotsky's) had much to do with the premise of their theories. Because his clubs and mentors engaged in scientific inquiry, Piaget would continue to believe that science was the tool by which he could create a rational epistemology. Because his activities and friends used social contact and language to inquire about truth and the human psyche, Vygotsky confirmed the sociocultural context of learning with language as its tool. All of these ideas were formed in their childhood and remained with them despite problems that occurred during what Americans would call their high school years (called gymnasium in parts of Europe).

GYMNASIUM OR ECOLE

Gymnasium (or Ecole) is often translated as high school, but it really is not. In Europe, the gymnasium/ecole is really at the level called college in America. In Europe, what Americans call the university is really postgraduate education. Both men excelled in their gymnasium studies, but both men also faced crises at this time. For Vygotsky, it was persecution. For Piaget, it was a second nervous breakdown. Both men, however, were able to overcome these difficulties and both graduated in the same year fully prepared to enter and excel at the university level.

Piaget

After graduating from the Latin School in 1911 with the highest marks in his class, Piaget entered the local ecole (gymnasium). Besides continued mentorship from Paul Godet, Piaget became closer to his godfather and uncle, Samuel Cornut. Cornut became a mentor along with two local teachers, Pierre Bovet and Arnold Reymond, who became acquainted with Jean Piaget in his gymnasium years because his father, Arthur, was a colleague at the local university.

Cornut, by introducing Piaget to evolutionary, free-thinking writers, caused Piaget to change his life's focus from science to epistemology. Bovet, as explained earlier, was founder and leader of the ACSE and rapidly developed a reputation as a gifted psychologist. Bovet, with his liberal Christian focus, would encourage Piaget to use psychology to help children. Godet taught with Piaget's two other major mentors (Bovet and Reymond) at the local gymnasium (before all three became university professors). Until 1896, the gymnasium was a branch of the university as a "sort of preparatory school" (Vidal, 1994, p. 16). It was divided into three sections: a literary or

Latin section prepared students for university entrance; a scientific section also prepared students for the university but was more focused on technical studies; and a pedagogical section that trained teachers at the primary level but was only two years instead of the usual three.

Piaget was to receive his baccalaureate in 1915 at the age of 18. His focus, at that time, was natural science. Godet, Bovet, and Reymond were important figures in his education but functioned in that capacity only outside of the classroom. The lesson of classroom teachers was not giving their students encouragement to pursue their own intellectual bent. This was not lost on Piaget. In 1954, he wrote a book so scathing against classroom education that it has yet to be published in America (Modgil, Modgil, & Brown, 1983). Piaget was unhappy with his formal education. Both at the Latin School and the local public gymnasium, teachers refused to allow children to pursue their own intellectual interests. If it were not for his challenging volunteer work under Godet and his older mentors, Piaget would have lost interest in academic endeavors. These mentors also stood with the young Piaget through two crises: one while at the gymnasium and one while in his first year at the university.

Piaget's abandonment of the religious zeal, expressed in 1915 with the essay *The Mission of the Idea*, bore an ironic relation to his growing independence from his mother and led to a new focus that was expressed in his first fictional novel, *Rescherere*, in which the hero, Sebastian, portrayed Piaget, himself abandoning religion in favor of science. Such an adjustment had a cost. While it was common for a person in Protestant Switzerland to go though a crisis of faith before deciding on Jesus, it was not common for that person to have a nervous breakdown (Sants, 1983).

The second nervous breakdown started when Piaget discovered a paper by Henri Bergson entitled *Creative Evolution* while browsing through his father's study. In it, Bergson used the idea of a hand going through compressed iron filings to suggest how nature produced complex organic structures. This illustration launched Piaget into an attempt to discover the evolution of thought. According to Piaget's four autobiographies, he first became acquainted with Bergson's thought after undergoing a course of religious instruction and reading the Protestant theologian Auguste Sabatier. Piaget's godfather, Samuel Cornut, gave him a copy of Sabatier's work *Outlines of a Philosophy of Religion Based on Psychology and History.* "He found me too specialized [in science] and wanted to teach me philosophy" (Piaget, 1952, p. 111). Sabatier argued that there was a difference between the moral essence of Christianity (conscience) and its historical expression (dogmas) and this implied that genuine faith is essentially a psychological phenomenon.

However, both Bergson and Sabatier were in conflict with what his mother and her church taught him. One of the results of this was that Piaget would develop a "silent hostility" (Vidal, 1994, p. 114) toward his mother. Another result was that Piaget would throw himself into his scientific studies at the Neuchatel Museum of Natural Science, which gave him some relief. However, Piaget would be caught in a conflict between his speculative and scientific sides for many years. His first novel, *Rescherche*, was printed in 1917 and dealt with the successful resolution of this conflict. In this novel, the hero decides that the only God that exists is the one within you and makes a decision to follow the scientific and rational over the philosophical and speculative.

Piaget's father asked him to read Kant in order to resolve his inner conflict (Rotman, 1977). Such a request resulted in Piaget's first research into rejecting popular philosophy with its irrationality. Jean Piaget became very skeptical of philosophy and any discipline that was not grounded in inductive reasoning. Piaget also came to believe that the study of biology could reconcile both science and religion. This was because "biology was the study of life and God could be identified with life itself" (Evans, 1922, pp. 108–111). So, by the time he was 16 years old, Piaget consecrated his life to the scientific explanation of how people think and acquire knowledge; in other words, he started to search for a rational epistemology.

Thus, Piaget had two crises: one of faith and one of the intellect. These led to two stays at Leysin, a tuberculosis sanitarium in the Swiss Alps: from September 1915 to April 1916 and from September 1916 to January 1917. The town's records only go back to 1920, so there is no official record of why he was there. Trying to cover up a mental breakdown, Piaget wrote to a friend that he had a case of measles that might threaten his lungs (Piaget, letter to Paul Pettavel, February 5, 1915). To explain her son's absence to curious neighbors who already felt that she was a difficult woman, his mother wrote that he had "a bad flu" (R. Piaget, letter to Paul Pettavel, May 17, 1916). There is no record of Piaget ever having tuberculosis, which was the excuse that Piaget's father gave to the neighbors. In fact, when in Leysin, "Piaget did not reside in a tuberculosis sanitarium but in two different pensions, Les Buits and Beau Soleil" (Vidal, 1994, p. 16). Piaget probably came the closest to the truth when he wrote to Arnold Reymond, "I was hurt, and retired into a nearby hill" (Piaget, letter to A. Reymond, October 5, 1918).

It was during this second visit to Leysin that Piaget resigned, citing "illness" (Piaget, letter to, September 25, 1915), from the Friends of Nature and wrote *Reschere* (Piaget, letter to Reymond, October 31, 1918).

Vygotsky

In Gomel, there were two gymnasiums. One was the official, public gymnasium. But the teachers there were "often extremely anti-Semitic"

(Dobkin, 1982, p. 28). This school was difficult to enter. A student had to pass a difficult series of tests and obtain the highest marks on them to get in. Also, the "quality of [instruction] lacking there left something to be desired" (Dobkin, 1982, p. 25). So, Vygotsky stayed with Ashpiz for 4 years and then sat for the examinations. He passed not only the fourth-form examinations but also the fifth and sixth. While enrolled in the public gymnasium, the obvious prejudice against Jews was too much for this sensitive student. Therefore, Vygotsky's parents pulled him out of that school and entered him in the Ratner's Gymnasium, a private Jewish school.

> It was then that he began to show the exciting peculiarities of his genius. He expressed great interest in all subjects and his abilities were such that each of his professors believed Vygotsky should follow his [that particular professor's] specialty. Thus, his mathematics professor predicted for him a brilliant future in that area, as did his Latin professor in the area of classical studies. (Blanck, 1990, p. 33)

Vygotsky graduated from the gymnasium in 1913 with the gold medal given only to the most outstanding Russian academic students. This should have guaranteed him a place at one of Russia's best universities, namely, the Imperial Moscow and St. Petersburg universities. But only 3 percent of all Jews in the empire could enter these universities by Imperical decree. To dilute the quality of Jews entering these universities, a lottery system began (Blanck, 1996; Dobkin, 1982; van der Veer & Valsiner, 1991; Wertsch, 1985). As Vygotsky was sitting for his required entrance examinations, the Czar had the Minister of Education start a new, stricter quota system. Although Vygotsky did not make a single mistake in his entrance examinations, his chances for entrance were now slim. This was a severe crisis in Vygotsky's life. Without a university education, he never could have created and published his cultural–historical theory.

> I remember sitting with Vygotsky on the porch of his dacha [our families rented dachas in Belitsa during the summer]. He had just washed his younger sister's feet, and read her some nursery rhymes of which he was very fond himself. (That summer I got to know him as a solicitous brother and considerate son.) Then he showed me the newspaper with the report about the new circular, which meant a great misfortune for him personally and for his whole family since it dashed his career plans and hopes of getting a university degree. "There," said Lev, "now I have no chance." The news seemed so monstrous to me that I replied: "If they don't admit you to the University it will be a terrible injustice. I am sure they'll let you in. Wanna bet?" Vygotsky, who was a great better, smiled and stretched out his hand. We happily discovered that he had obtained entrance to the Imperial Moscow University. Unlike Piaget, Vygotsky's formal education was excellent and prepared him well for his university years. Vygotsky knew by that time

that his main interest was already orientated toward drama, literature and philosophy. (Blanck, 1990, p. 2)

Conclusion

Both Piaget and Vygotsky studied at the best gymnasiums in town. Nevertheless, this time of their youth, which should have been enjoyable and happy, was really a time of crises for both. They did not succumb to the crises, but, instead, conquered them. The methods that they used to help themselves overcome their difficulties would result in each teenager being convinced that there was a better way to educate people. One either needed to reform it intellectually (Piaget) or find a better social means of instruction (Vygotsky).

CHAPTER 3

YOUNG ADULTHOOD

INTRODUCTION

Vygotsky's and Piaget's original ambitions, which were clearly not abandoned until after the college years, were different from what they would eventually become. Piaget wanted to be a biologist and Vygotsky enjoyed literature and philology (the study of language). Then, fate stepped in and changed their goals. Already known as bright, talented students, it seemed that both were destined to leave the world a better place. Their university years formed the final learning stage for their respective pedagogies. During this time, they would find names to go with their ideas. Later, during their postgraduate work, they would test out those ideas and find them sound. However, just as their gymnasium/ecole years were not peaceful, so too were their days at the university.

Both graduated from the university within 2 years of each other. Both changed their focus of study to psychology while at the university. Both had their focus of research affected by World War I.

UNIVERSITY YEARS

It was at the university that both Piaget and Vygotsky were able to take courses that showed them their individual ideas could be put into one, conclusive pedagogy. In addition, terms could be given to those ideas; thus, it was at the university that all the ideas composed within their minds

Parallel Paths to Constructivism: Jean Piaget and Lev Vygotsky, pages 37–44
Copyright © 2004 by Information Age Publishing

came together. The ability of these two men to be so flexible as to change fields of study is partly attributable to the fact that this was made possible by their respective countries' university structures.

At the university, both Piaget and Vygotsky were introduced for the first time to psychology as a possible future career. This was because psychology, at that time, was considered part of both men's primary field of study. The two young men received baccalaureates from leading colleges within 2 years of each other. Piaget graduated from the University of Neuchatel in 1918 with a doctorate in the natural sciences. He could have had a doctorate also in philosophy (he had taken all the courses), but he did not submit a dissertation. Piaget then studied philosophy and epistemology for a semester at the University of Zurich, where he picked up an interest in psychoanalysis, which he was later to reject. Vygotsky received two degrees simultaneously from the Imperial University in Moscow (law and literary analysis) and Shanaivsky University (history and philosophy) in 1917. Psychology was considered part of philosophy by the Swiss university and psychology was considered part of history and philology by Shanyavsky University and the Imperial University in Moscow.

Piaget

Piaget studied natural science at the University of Neuchatel. Just as in his elementary and ecole years, most of his learning took place outside the formal classroom—courtesy of outside and older mentors who helped the young man mature intellectually. One of those was an earlier mentor, Professor Arnold Reymond, from whom Piaget learned more out of the classroom than in it.

It was Reymond who encouraged Piaget in his idea to purge the irrational from philosophy. While the idea was started in Piaget's ecole years, this decision was finalized in Piaget's university years. It was Reymond who was to provide the final link with which Piaget could fuse the rational thinking of biology with philosophy. This was provided by a lesson Reymond gave on realism and monimalism "within the problem of universals," and it "gave me a sudden insight" (Piaget, 1976, in Evans, 1981, p. 113). This link did not occur until Piaget had time to reflect on Reymond's lesson while recuperating for the second time at Leysin. He spent more than a year in the mountains writing "a sort of philosophic novel which I was imprudent enough to publish in 1917" (Piaget, 1952, p.112).

> I began to read everything which came into my hands after my unfortunate contact with the philosophy of Bergson: some Kant, Spencer, Auguste Comte, Fouillee and Guyau Lachelier, Boutroux, Lalande, Durkheim, Tarde, Le Dantec; and, in psychology, W. James, Th. Ribot, and Janet. Also, during

the last two years before the baccalaureate, we had lessons in psychology, in logic, and in scientific methodology given by the logician, A. Reymond. But for lack of a laboratory (their was no experimental psychologist at Neuchatel, even at the university) the only thing I could do was to theorize and write. (Piaget, 1952, in Evans, 1981, pp. 112–113)

The personal steps that Piaget went through in order to reach this decision gave birth to two ideas: (a) his theory of equilibration and (b) the concept that the only God that existed was the one within you. In other words, Piaget internalized God much as he had his students internalize constructs. By August 1917, Piaget rejected the personalized Jesus of his youthful *Mission of the Idea* in favor of a more rational approach to philosophy. "He asserted the vanity of all intellectual metaphysics, claimed to have got rid of metaphysics and theology, and characterized the problem that made up his life as that of basing morality on science" (Piaget, 1917, in Vidal, 1994, p. 161). The result of this was that Piaget would write *Recherches [sur la Contradiction]* in 1918.

Rescherches was for Piaget an extended self-evaluation and search for truth. "You can make life's little irritations disappear by burying yourself in your work" (Piaget, 1918/1980, p. 4). Piaget attempted to find a scientific explanation for the development of human knowledge. In this work, the hero extricates himself from emotional chaos by setting himself to work. Thus, Piaget discovered that work and science allowed him to free himself from neurosis that had worried him since childhood and that he feared would make him insane. It was the result of introspective self-examination produced by the enforced idleness and quiet of Leysin.

In the Swiss-French Protestant milieu, "formation novels appeared as the ideal means of communicating the results of introspective self-examination, especially in relation to the processes of conversion deemed to be the foundation of faith" (Vidal, 1994, p. 183). Sebastian, the hero of *Rescherches*, ends up rejecting a personal God in favor of science, but it is science that requires a rational faith. God was transcendent and was within everything and everywhere. It took scientific observation to find Him. For Piaget, the most important contribution of science to salvation was that it showed the interdependence of morality, religion, and education (Vidal, 1994).

Education led to the establishment of social reforms aimed at the equilibration of society itself. Piaget may have incorporated his theory of equilibrium into this novel to avoid compromising himself on scientific grounds. Piaget saw himself as a "militant philosopher" (Piaget, letter to Reymond, 1924). He aimed the ideas in *Rescherche* to his peers and those among the public who sought intellectual illumination. In his 1954 autobiography, Piaget said that during the time he spent in the mountains,

I was haunted by the desire to create, and I yielded to the temptation. Not to compromise myself on scientific grounds, however, I avoided the difficulty by writing—for the general public, and not for specialists—a kind of philosophic novel, the last part which contained my ideas. My strategy proved to be correct: No one spoke of it except one or two indignant philosopher. (1954, p. 116)

Vygotsky

Starting in 1914, Vygotsky attended two universities at the same time; namely, the Imperial University in Moscow and Shanyavsky Peoples' University in Moscow. His faith determined the choice of subject. While his parents wanted him to study medicine, he quickly switched after one month to law (van der Veer & Valsiner, 1991). This was because the only Jews who could live outside of the Pale of Settlement (the geographical boundaries where Jews could live in Russia as determined by the Czar) were Jewish lawyers. Law was an option "more suited to his interest in the humanities" (Blanck, 1990, p. 34). Vygotsky actually wanted to study history and philology (the study of language). However, these only led to a teaching career and, as a Jew, he could not be a government employee (i.e., teacher) (Blanck, 1990).

Shanyavsky University sprang up in 1911 after the Minister of Education Kasso (because anti-czarist movements) expelled most of the students at the Imperial (Moscow) University. Over a hundred professors walked out in protest. Most of them were the best professors at Moscow University. While there was no department of history and philosophy at Moscow University, there was one at the newly formed Shanyavsky. "To indulge himself," Vygotsky started taking courses. While this university was a school "of the highest standards," its "degree was unofficial, not recognized by the czarist government, and gave no rights to its holders" (Dobkin, 1982, p. 29).

At Shanyavsky University, Vygotsky's interests broadened to include psychological and pedagogical problems (van der Veer & Valsiner, 1991). His sister joined him after 2 years. Together, they took a course from Dr. Gustav Shpet on the "internal form of the word" (Mitjushin, 1988; Shpet, 1927). This course "gave them sensitivity to the internal and psychological aspects of language" (van der Veer & Valsiner, 1991, p. 8). Around this time, Vygotsky also started reading the work of James and Freud. "It can be argued that Vygotsky's liking for these books revealed an interest in the extreme layers of mind and...a predilection for speculative studies" (van der Veer & Valsiner, 1991, p. 8). The thought that language was a tool of learning was starting to form in Vygotsky's mind.

Moscow was an exciting place for Vygotsky. Innovative trends in the sciences, humanities, and arts emerged. Vygotsky seemed to keenly pursue them all (Kozulin, 1986). Since the highest intellects were at Shanyavsky

University, Vygotsky obtained a solid foundation in history, philosophy, and psychology, and pursued studies in literature, "which continued to be his primary interest" (Blanck, 1990, p. 35).

"Vygotsky gained much more from the atmosphere at that University and from mixing with the students and teachers there than from his studies at the law department [at Moscow University]" (Dobkin, 1982, p. 30). At Shanaivsky, psychology was taught as part of literary analysis and philosophy. So, this opened the door for Vygotsky to become a psychologist. He would graduate from Shanaivsky in 1917 with a degree in history and literary analysis. That same year, he also obtained his law and philology degrees from Moscow University, but he never became a lawyer. His doctorate in literary analysis was awarded after he defended his dissertation, *The History of the Idea*, which was a literary analysis of *Hamlet*. Because of an attack of tuberculosis, he was allowed to graduate before he defended it. He successfully defended his dissertation in 1924. By 1917, the Russian Revolution had started and he was now able to become a teacher due to the abolition of anti-Semitic legislation (Carr, 1967). However, his law studies did have an impact on him.

Dobkin remembered, "his studies at the law department helped Vygotsky develop his gift of oratory, although I must say that he had a knack for expressing his ideas clearly and convincingly from childhood" (Dobkin, 1982, p. 30). Now, he could make anything sound exciting and interesting. That virtue helped Vygotsky to speak without notes and, at the same time, exert a charismatic personality. His oratory impressed listeners in 1924 so much that Luria said, after hearing Vygotsky at the Second Psychoneurological Congress, that he got Kornilov to invite Vygotsky to Moscow, and a new career in pedagogy began for Vygotsky due to his oratorical ability (Luria, 1979).

Conclusion

It was at the university that the possibility of changing careers opened up to both men. Piaget, dedicated earlier to natural science, would start to switch to epistemology, which is the heart of philosophy. Vygotsky, with philology and law degrees from Moscow University and two degrees from Shanyvasky University, would observe that the door to becoming a pedagogist was open to him. Both would make this observation because their universities made psychology part of the curriculum of both men's original field of study. However, the final switch would not be made until World War I.

WORLD WAR I

World War I had outward effects on Vygotsky and inward effects on Piaget. The deprivations of both the war and Russian Revolution coming hard upon each other would weaken Vygotsky's already slight physique and increase his fatalism. Its deprivations caused Vygotsky to contract tuberculosis from his younger brother. The sufferings that Piaget escaped but witnessed led him to question the existence of a personal God, renunciation of organized religion, and a desire to purge philosophy of its irrational nature (Piaget, 1976).

Piaget

Piaget's mother became involved in helping wounded and captured soldiers on both sides of World War I and securing their humane treatment in Switzerland. Sometimes Piaget went along with his mother on her rounds of inquiry. In December, influenced by the suffering of World War I, Piaget wrote the *Mission of the Idea* and the Swiss Christian Students' Association published it. This was a prose poem in which Piaget proclaimed that the mission of youth was to work toward the renewal of Christianity and the creation of a better world out of the ruins of World War I. In it, Piaget considered the possibility that moral concepts can evolve. That thought was crucial to his intellectual development, and this would later let him attempt to provide evolutionary ethics with scientific foundations.

Piaget was clearly against the war and saw it as a consequence of unbendable orthodoxy (Vidal, 1994). In the poem, Piaget called for a renewal of Christianity in such a way as to make a better world. The poem "stated Piaget's earliest metaphysics and it is within the context of the system of the Idea [to produce a better world] that Piaget started to assert his religious and social outlook" (Vidal, 1994, p. 133). This would also happen for Vygotsky.

Vygotsky

World War I had grave consequences for Vygotsky. The terrible conflict contained within it the bloody Russian Revolution. The Russian people suffered horribly from both. There is an old Russian greeting that asks, "Have you suffered well today?" (L. McClendon, personal communication, June 24, 1998). In their long history, the Russian people have faced many difficult times. The horrors of both World War I and the Russian Revolution made the second decade of the century very difficult. That difficulty was only exceeded by the larger, and more bloody, World War II. This decade was so difficult for Vygotsky that he never really talked about it, even to his children. All they knew was that Vygotsky's brother died, Vygotsky and his mother were stuck in Kiev without income for more than several months (Vygodskaya, 1994).

First, there were economic deprivations. Food and fuel were scarce. Without enough to eat and little warmth during the very cold Russian winters, many citizens became sick and died. Already of slight build, Vygotsky's younger brother, Dodik, fell ill with tuberculosis. The nearest sanitarium was too near the fighting and, anyway, conditions were not any better there than at the Vygodsky apartment. Although his family understood how contagious the disease was, they did not desert him. To save his life, and take him far from the fighting, Lev and his mother tried to take Dodik to the warmer and safer climate of the Crimea. University students were not drafted into the Imperial army and Jews were not trusted by the Czar Nicholas as soldiers, so Vygotsky left his studies and went with them, but they could get no farther than Kiev.

In Kiev, Vygotsky had a hard time getting enough for his mother and brother to eat. The city was full of refugees and jobs were scarce. People who could find jobs were employed in work that they were not trained for. A.N. Leontiev once wrote that knowledge of Vygotsky's personality is necessary to understand his work (Vygodaskaya, 1994). It was in Kiev, in deep depression after his brother's death and in intense anxiety and frustration (no work, no income, and no way to get back home) that Vygotsky decided to be like others in Kiev and change careers. At the time, there was no employment for lawyers or literary critics (he had his university degrees in both). Instead, he would become a teacher.

The Russian Revolution was considered a major turning point of the 20th century (Carr, 1967). A.R. Luria (1979) wrote that the Revolution radically changed major fields of study, including psychology. Whole new realms of inquiry were opened and "opportunities for younger scholars were greater than had been previously imaginable" (Wertsch, 1985, p. 7). Despite the hardships and deaths, the Revolution allowed Vygotsky to become a pedagogist. This is because, once he became a teacher, he was so respected that he was asked to teach at the local teachers' college. The combination of jobs made him think about building an educational psychology laboratory. Now, the ideas that were planted in his childhood, grew in his adolescence, and became tied together at the university could be proven true or false. The research done in the Gomel laboratory, however, proved them true.

Conclusion

Both men would pay a price for World War I. With Piaget, the cost was psychological. He had two nervous breakdowns for which wartime was at least partly responsible because it demonstrated that mankind needed something higher than illogical psychological forces to depend upon (Piaget, 1918). For Vygotsky, the cost was higher. He lost a brother and contracted a disease that would eventually take his life. However, both men translated these difficulties into creative work. Piaget would write two works that showed a change in his life, namely, from Christianity to Deism and a resolve to purge philosophy of its irrational aspects through use of scientific logic. Vygotsky would change fields of study. Instead of becoming a lawyer, he would become a teacher and, eventually, a psychologist. So it was at the university that both Piaget and Vygotsky realized that they could make a major contribution to the world by giving the world the ideas that they had conceived in childhood.

Each tried his hand briefly at a practical approach to his university education before leaving that to spend the rest of his career in research. Piaget diagnosed learning disorders for a few years in Paris and Vygotsky taught in a public high school for 7 years in Gomel. As Piaget observed his ideas correct in Paris and, later, at the Jean-Jacques Rousseau Institute in Geneva, and as Vygotsky's research proved his ideas correct at both the public high school and teachers' college in Gomel, both felt empowered with the truth. During the 1920s, the result of both postgraduate jobs guaranteed their ascents, which took them to the peaks of pedagogy midway through the 20th century.

CHAPTER 4

POSTGRADUATE WORK

INTRODUCTION

When it came to setting out their ideas, the postgraduate work of Piaget and Vygotsky was the most important phase of their lives. Indeed, when considering its part in the creation of their respective learning theories, it is only second to their childhood experiences. It was their postgraduate work that polished their ideas and provided the research that proved those ideas correct. They both started their postgraduate work within a year of each other. They also both wrote a major work of pedagogy that gave them national notice in 1924.

Interestingly enough, both married within a year of each other. In addition, Piaget and Vygotsky had three children. Each man had a child born in 1924, 1927, and 1931. Two daughters were born first, and both in the same year. A son followed for both fathers and both sons were born in 1931. Piaget's son survived him, but Vygotsky's son died in infancy. Piaget's wife, whom he married in 1923, was an educational researcher and Vygotsky's wife, whom he married in 1924, was a teacher. Both their wives and their children encouraged both men to research pedagogy further. Both wives assisted in their men's pedagogical research as both men observed their children's activities, which were, in reality, research experiments.

Both men left their postgraduate jobs within a year of each other. Vygotsky left in 1924 to become a junior research assistant at Kornilov's institute for psychological research in Moscow. By 1926, he had formed the Moscow "troika" (group of three) with Luria and Leontiev, wrote *The His-*

Parallel Paths to Constructivism: Jean Piaget and Lev Vygotsky, pages 45–55
Copyright © 2004 by Information Age Publishing

torical Meaning of the Crisis in Psychology, and became a department head. Piaget's mentor Sabatier died and recommended Piaget to his post. Piaget then became professor of psychology, sociology, and the philosophy of science at the University of Neuchatel in 1925. Piaget wrote his noteworthy books 2 and 3 years ahead of Vygotsky, who was struggling with a second bout of tuberculosis at the time. Piaget wrote *Language and Thought of the Child* in 1923 and *Judgment and Reasoning of the Child* in 1924. Both books were to have a profound impact on Vygotsky's theory.

Piaget

After graduating from the University of Neuchatel in 1918 with a doctorate in natural sciences, Piaget left for the University of Zurich. He studied psychology under professors Lipps and Wreschner. In addition, he also worked at Dr. Bleuler's psychiatric clinic. "I felt at once that there lay my path," remembered Piaget (1964, p. 117). Earlier, "The teachings of Bleuler made me sense the danger of solitary meditation," and Piaget decided to reject psychoanalysis "lest I should fall a victim to 'autism'" (1964, p. 117). Piaget went to le Valais in the spring of 1919 to finish a taxonomy of mollusks that he had begun while at the Museum of Natural History in Neuchatel but had to forego in favor of his academic studies. He applied Lipp's statistical method to the biometrics study of the variability of land mollusks as a function of altitude because "I needed to get back to concrete problems to avoid grave [i.e., mental] errors" (1964, p. 118).

Part of the choice to get back to concrete problems meant leaving Switzerland for Paris. There, Piaget became the student of Pierre Janet, for whom he would later write a complimentary biography and call him his "true mentor" (Piaget, in Amman-Gainotti, 1992, p. 1012). From Janet, Piaget picked up a genetic approach to the psychology of behavior. He also honed his ideas about the hierarchical organization of psychological functions while working in Janet's laboratory. Observations that Piaget had made in his youth while looking at mollusks and snails in the laboratory now came together under the focus of Dr. Janet. The seed planted in the Neuchatel museum to create a theory about chronological stages of cognitive development now sprung forth fully developed in Janet's lab.

Janet had started developing the idea that Piaget would later finish developing and call equilibration; that is, a child observed, internalized that observation, and then created a construct from this internalization. This verbalized what Piaget had gone through during his two mental breakdowns and endorsed his idea of equilibration that he wrote about in *Recherches [Sur le Contradition]* in 1918.

Janet's generic approach to the psychology of behavior also provided Piaget with a conceptual framework within which to work and develop

Piaget's own project of studying the formation of knowledge. Janet also influenced Vygotsky. "From Janet, Vygotsky received the idea that interpersonal processes can transform into interpersonal ones" (Blanck, 1990, p. 47).

> While working with Dr. Janet, Piaget also spent two years at the Sorbonne. I attended Dumas' course in pathological psychology (where I learned to interview mental patients at Sainte-Anne), and the courses of Pieron and Delacroix; I also studied logic and philosophy of science with Lalande and Brunschwieg. The latter exerted a great influence on me because of his historical-critical method and his references to psychology. (Piaget, in Evans, 1981, p. 118)

When Dr. Binet died, Dr. Simon invited Piaget to use Binet's laboratory at the grade school named rue de la Grange aux Belles. Dr. Simon, living in Rouen, could not use the laboratory. Dr. Simon asked Piaget to standardize Dr. Burt's reasoning tests on the children. "I had an extraordinary piece of luck. I started the work without much enthusiasm, just to try anything. But soon my mood changed; there I was, my own master, with a whole school at my disposition—unhoped [sic] for working conditions" (Piaget, in Evans, 1981, p. 118). Piaget soon became more interested in the failures than the successes with the diagnostic test. Remembering his questioning experience at Sainte-Anne, Piaget started talking to his subjects. He became intrigued when he discovered that children up to the age of 11 or 12 had unsuspected learning difficulties in three areas: coordination of relations, multiplication of classes, and inclusion of a part in a whole.

Without Dr. Simon suspecting it, Piaget continued for about 2 years to work with both normal children and children with learning problems at Salpetriere. "At last, I had found my field of research," exclaimed Piaget (in Evans, 1981, p. 119). With his knowledge of Gestalt, Piaget said that it became clear to him that the theory of the relations between the whole and the part can

> be studied experimentally through analysis of the psychological processes underlying logical operations. This marked the end of my theoretical period and the start of an inductive and experimental era in the psychological domain which I always had wanted to enter, but for which until then I had not found the suitable problems. (in Evans, 1981, pp. 119–120)

Piaget remembered his studies of Bergson and decided that, by his observations, logic was not inborn but develops consistently with his idea of equilibration. He also believed that he should study the problem of logic and discover "a sort of embryology of intelligence" (Piaget in Evans, 1981, p. 120). All three of these ideas melded his interests in biology and philosophy. The research on these ideas resulted in three articles. These articles were based on Piaget's new ideas. "I analyzed the data, psychologically as well as logically, applying the principle of logical-psychological parallelism to my method of analysis: Psychology explains the facts in terms of causality, while logic when concerned with true reasoning described the corresponding forms in terms of an ideal equilibrium" (in Evans, 1981, p. 120).

Journal de Psychologie published two of the three articles and its editor became Piaget's friend. Editor I. Meyerson spurred Piaget on with his encouragement and advice. The third article was sent to Piaget's old mentor, Edouard Claparede, who published it in *The Archives de Psychologie*. Claparede also offered Piaget a job as director of studies at the Jean-Jacques Rousseau Institute in Geneva. Piaget came to Geneva

> for a month's trial. This prospect enchanted me, as much because of Claparede's fame as for the wonderful research facilities which this position would afford; on the other hand, as yet I did not know how to start out on any research! I accepted in principle, and...I noted immediately that Claparede and Bovet were ideal patrons who would let me work according to my desires. (in Evans, 1981, p. 121)

Arriving in 1921 to work at the Jean-Jacques Rousseau Institute, Piaget finished conceptualizing and synthesizing his pedagogical ideas through formal research. Claparede and Pierre Bovet (Piaget's mentors at this institute) were "deeply committed Protestants, and much of their cognitive and moral universe overlapped with that of Piaget even before he became Claparede's and Bovet's colleague at the Rousseau Institute in 1921" (Vidal, 1994, p. 101).

At the Rousseau Institute, Piaget researched his ideas in a school laboratory and found them correct. The Institute had an activity school as part of its laboratory, where students were free to create their own learning situations in an intellectually stimulating environment (R. Colet, personal communication, March 29, 1998).

At the Rousseau Institute, all of Piaget's ideas came together. His earlier research in Paris proved correct as he worked in Claparede's activity school. Piaget's work consisted of guiding the students and associating with them while doing his own child psychology research. Piaget started by researching peripheral factors such as social environment and language. His goal was to find the psychological mechanism of logical operations and causal reasoning.

Vygotsky

After graduation from both Moscow and Shanyavsky University in 1917, Vygotsky returned to Gomel. There, he taught school, took a course, created a psychological laboratory, wrote his first book, started a family, began his psychological research, and contributed to Gomel's culture.

Although he had degrees from two universities, Vygotsky made the time to take a course from Vladimir Uzin in Gomel. Uzin had no formal education and was quite a bit older than Vygotsky. However, he was very intelligent and self-educated. A polyglot, he was particularly good at Latin and Spanish. After the Russian Revolution, he wrote many works on literary criticism. He also translated Spanish drama and literature into Russian, wrote essays on drama, and wrote a foreword to the Russian edition of Lope de Vega's plays (Dobkin, 1982). Whatever endorsement Vygotsky further needed to understand language was a tool of learning, he received from Uzin. Also, this work prepared Vygotsky for writing the introduction to the Russian edition of Piaget's *Language and Thought of the Child* (1923).

Vygotsky was very busy in Gomel after his brother's death in 1918. Perhaps Vygotsky kept himself busy because, by 1919, he knew that he had tuberculosis and, with his fatalism, believed that it would one day kill him. He had a legacy to leave and feverishly worked to create it. In addition, hard work keeps one's mind too busy to focus on the death of a loved one or revolutionary chaos (Gomel was in the midst of fighting at this time). To earn some income, Vygotsky and his cousin David started teaching literature at the local public high school in late 1918 (Dobkin, 1982). Lev was to spend 7 years in Gomel teaching at this school.

Vygotsky picked up his ideas for cultural–historical theory during his youth in Gomel. However, it was not until working as a public high school teacher in Gomel that he researched these ideas, discovered that he was correct, and published his first work, telling the world about his new pedagogy.

While Vygotsky was busy instructing high school students, he was also busy teaching education courses to would-be instructors. Vygotsky taught at the Gomel Teacher College or Pedagogicheske Uchilishche. There, he built his first psychological laboratory. The techniques he used in the Gomel public high school were scrutinized in this laboratory. This was to play "a major role in Vygotsky's development as a scientist" (van der Veer & Valsiner, 1991, p. 9). Vygotsky and his student teachers performed simple but practical investigations. In this laboratory they performed experiments on reactions that provided the material for his famous address before the 1924 Second Psychoneurological Congress (Vygotsky, 1926), it also resulted in his first major book, *Pedagogological Psychology*, which was published in 1926 (Wertsch, 1985). This 1924 speech earned him a "modest position as junior staff scientist" (Wertsch, 1985, p. 10) at Kornilov's institute for psychology in Moscow.

It was with *Pedagogological Psychology* that Vygotsky joined Marx's dialectical with language as a tool of learning and put both in a cultural–historical context. It was during his 7 years in Gomel that Vygotsky decided to become a Soviet. Vygotsky saw Leninism as liberating and he needed a theory to prove Marx correct. His work at the Gomel laboratory cemented Marxist theory and his first book proclaimed it. He was "eager to lay the foundations of a Marxist psychology [that]...developed...from practice in the young Soviet land. Theory was a means and not an end. He was anxious to make his contribution to the great transformations taking place in the Soviet state" (Dobkin, 1982, p. 9).

Vygotsky also taught at various other institutes in the Gomel area. For example, he taught at the Soviet Labor School or Sovetskaja Trudovaja Shkola. He taught at the Evening School for Adult Workers, the Rabfak. This was a school designed to give blue-collar adults a chance at a university education by providing them with preparatory courses first. He also taught at the Kursy Podgotovki Pedagogov. The subjects Vygotsky taught ranged from literature and language to logic, psychology, and pedagogy. He taught courses in aesthetics and art history at the local conservatory, and in theater at a local studio.

Vygotsky also managed to contribute a great deal to Gomel's culture. He founded his publishing firm "Ages of Days." With its publication of Ilya Ehrenburg's book *Fire*, Vygotsky "got his start" at becoming known" (Levitin, 1982, p. 10). Vygotsky also set up literature lectures for the townsfolk that he called "Literary Mondays." (Blanck, 1982, p. 36). At these Mondays, Vygotsky's talks focused on a wide range of writings. He spoke on such authors as Shakespeare, Goethe, Pushkin, Chekhov, Mayakovsky, and Esenin. He even spoke on Einstein's theory of relativity, something that few scientists understood at the time. "Vygotsky's brilliant lectures attracted large audiences" (Kolvanovsky, in Levitin, 1982, p. 388).

In addition, Vygotsky was one of the founders of a literary magazine entitled *Veresk*. He also edited and published articles in the theater section of the Gomel newspaper (Vygodskaya, 1984). Zinaida Vygodsky once said that she did not think "that there was any period in his life when he did not think or write about the theater" (Davydov, in Levitin, 1982, p. 20). Finally, Vygotsky somehow found time for reading works that he considered recreational. Among the authors that he read at this time were Tyuchev, Bliok, Mandel'shtam, Pushkin, Tolstoy, Dostoevsky, Bely, Bunin, James, Spinoza, Freud, Marx, Engels, Hegel, Pavlov, and Potebnya (Wertsch, 1985).

Despite a hectic schedule, Vygotsky also managed to finish his doctoral dissertation and got married in 1924. After submitting his dissertation, *The Psychology of Art*, Vygotsky asked for a public defense but was thwarted in this when his tuberculosis put him back in the sanitarium. His committee, therefore, waved the defense and Vygotsky's dissertation was approved. In 1924 while in the sanitarium, Vygotsky read a book that Piaget published in 1923, *Le Judgement et le raisonment chez infant.* This formed a culmination of thought that Lev had in his mind as he observed the stages of development both in literature and in people. Now, he knew that there were stages to educational development; however, he disagreed with Piaget that these could be set by specific chronological age groupings.

On January 6, 1924, Vygotsky delivered three papers at the Second Psychoneurological Congress in Leningrad. He spoke without notes, but very fluently. The Experimental Psychological Institute (Kornilov Institute) in Moscow was looking for a way to prove Marxism correct and, at the same time, combat the behaviorists and empiricists. Vygotsky's presentation on *Methods of Reflexological and Psychological Investigations* met that need. At age 28, having already endured two hospitalizations for tuberculosis, Vygotsky tackled their problem with a notable and persuasive address. "It was clear that this man from a small provincial town in western Russia was an intellectual force who would have to be listened to" (Luria, 1979, p. 39). Lenin's widow, N.K. Krupskaya, was Deputy Minister of Art and Education. Anatoli Lunacharsky was Minister of Art and Education. Together, they wanted to more fully utilize the talents of intelligent pedagogists to reform Soviet education (Prawat, 2002). After his 1924 address, Danjushevsky requested that both ministers bring Vygotsky to Moscow. Krupskaya and Lunacharsky agreed and Vygotsky came.

In summation, it was the Gomel period that marked Vygotsky's decision to change fields and become a psychologist (van der Veer & Valsiner, 1991). This shift was a gradual one. What induced it? Semyon Dobkin believed that it was Vygotsky's interest in fiction that made him switch careers and become a psychologist. "In part, the turn to that science [psychology] was a natural corollary of his interest in fiction, notably the psychological novel. At the same time, his acquaintance with some scholarly works quickened his interest in the subject" (Dobkin, 1982, p. 33).

Others disagree with Dobkin. While literature "always gave him much solace and always engaged his attention...the underlying basis of all his concepts was the Marxist philosophy to which he pledged fealty" (Davydov, 1967, p. 20). Dr. Stephen Toulmin, professor of Social Thought and Philosophy at the University of Chicago, said that it was Vygotsky's early exposure to Marx that made him tackle the problems of child development "in his own original way" (Toulmin, in Levitin, 1982, p. 20).

All historians writing in the thesis school on Lev Vygotsky would agree with Toulmin. Many Russian intellectuals at the time wanted to see the Communist Revolution succeed (Davydov & Radzikhjovsky, 1985; Yaroshevsky, 1994, 1996; Zaporozhetz, 1967). Georgy Schedrovitsky, a prominent Soviet methodologist with a special interest in the history of psychology, said that it did not matter what catalyst made Vygotsky publish cultural–historical theory. The important factor to focus on was that he was great because he was not a professional psychologist by formal training. So, from the start, Vygotsky was free of the limitations of any of the dominant schools of psychology at the time (Schedrovitsky, in Levitin, 1982).

MARRIAGE

Perhaps it is interesting to note that Vygotsky and Piaget married within a year of each other. Each one chose as his wife a future collaborator and helper as well as a lover and friend. In addition, both wives were self-effacing; that is, they sought no glory for themselves but served as helpers for their gifted but driven husbands. With both husbands being workaholics, the everyday task of bringing up a family lay on the shoulders of these wives. Both were known for good humor and a positive outlook. Valentine bore three children for her husband and this moved Piaget to change from child psychology to pedagogy because now he had the chance to observe the impact of his educational ideas upon his own children.

Piaget's Wife

Collaborating with Piaget in his postgraduate work was a young, attractive student named Valentine Chatenay. They married in 1923 and she "became my wife and constant co-worker" (Piaget, in Evans, 1981, p. 123). Pictures of Valentine reveal her to be an attractive and pleasant young lady. Piaget guarded his private life well and wrote little describing his wife and marriage. Piaget published five books on child psychology as a result of his research with her support while at the Jean-Jacques Rousseau Institute. However, he did not think that many people would read them, and was pleasantly surprised when many people did and he was invited to many countries to explain his ideas. Having no children yet, Piaget remembered that, at the time, he "had no interest in pedagogy" (Piaget, in Evans, 1981, p. 123).

That was to change in 1925 when Piaget became a father. It is known that Valentine continued to help Piaget with his research, especially when that research concerned their three children. She also served as critic for Piaget's works. A daughter, Jacqueline, was born in 1925 (the same year Vygotsky's daughter Gita was born). Another daughter, Lucienne was born in 1927 (the same year Vygotsky's daughter, Asya was born). A son, Laurent, was born in 1931.

Vygotsky's Wife

During 1923, Vygotsky began to court a pretty local girl named Roza Noevna Smekhova. Dobkin described her as "a vivacious, intelligent, pretty girl. She had a gift for staying cheerful throughout the many difficult situations in which they found themselves" (Dobkin, 1982, p. 37). Vygotsky married Roza but not much is known about her either. She is described as a good-humored, determined, intelligent, and attractive young lady (Blanck, 1990; Dobkin, 1982).

Roza was a schoolteacher but she quit her job upon their move to Moscow in 1924. It was in that year that Vygotsky delivered his now-famous address to the Second Psychoneurological Congress that won him a ticket to Moscow. For 10 years in Moscow, Lev and Roza shared a one-room basement apartment with their children, mother-in-law, four sisters-in-law, and one brother-in-law. Although already overcrowded, the Vygotsky apartment "doubled as an archive for his department's philosophical section" (Levitin, 1982, p. 37). Vygotsky's students would often come to the apartment at the end of the day to debate with him on questions that interested them. Often there was not enough food or fuel. Despite this, Roza, Vygotsky's wife, was never known to utter an angry word (Vygodskaya, 1994/1996). Vygotsky put in many extra hours working for the Educational Psychological Institute, but she never uttered a public complaint. "The family was ruled by the spirit of love and mutual respect" (Vygodskaya, 1994/1996, p. 2). After Vygotsky's death, she showed her strength of character. Roza often worked up to 16 hours a day taking care of handicapped children (Blanck, 1990). She and Lev had three children. Asya died in 1985 but not before becoming a specialist in biophysics. Gita Levovna Vygodskaya was an educational psychologist. She is now retired, living in Moscow, and has published three works on her father. According to Gita, there was a son who died in infancy (Vygodskaya, 1994). Vygotsky, like Piaget, did research by observing his children: "We with my brother would permanently be father's test objects and we liked it when he introduced us to his experiments" (Vygodskaya, 1994, p. 3).

Conclusion

The freedom that both men enjoyed in their postgraduate work resulted in prolific and notable contributions that were first published in 1924. However, the true scope of their theories would not become obvious to the world until after they started their professional careers in 1925.

The result of Piaget's and Vygotsky's trials would be that both would endure repeated crises of depression. As a preventative measure against such attacks, both would become workaholics and use their intellects to conquer their emotional trauma. A tribute to the sheer stamina of each man's public contributions to pedagogy and to the complexities of his character was that each man was able to overcome his problems. The methods by which he did so helped form the basis of his learning theory.

Neither one relished the prospect of proving themselves courageous heroes but the personal tragedies in their lives led to them becoming forceful, skillful men who could successfully counteract the noted theories of their time (mainly empiricism, Gestalt, and behavioralism).

Although Piaget was set to become a natural scientist and Vygotsky a teacher, it was a combination of both their characters and the events that surrounded them that caused them to shift careers and, thus, the focus of their life's work. For both men, the decision to dedicate their lives to intellectual ideas was to inject strength of character into their later careers.

Their work at their respective institutes only confirmed through formal research and publications the ideas that were formulated in their childhood and proven informally correct in their postgraduate endeavors by work in Janet's and Binet's labs (Piaget) or the Gomel high school and teachers' college (Vygotsky).

EPILOGUE

Their intellectual prowess, academic training, and gift for scholarly inquiry had put them in definite positions to grasp and wield change in the world's belief on how people think and can be taught. All the difficulties, all the people, all the events of their lives seemed to come together to weave important ideas that would significantly contribute to children's education.

Piaget

In 1925, Arnold Reymond retired from his position as chair of philosophy at the University of Neuchatel. He recommended Piaget as his replacement. Piaget accepted and taught psychology, the philosophy of science, sociology, and a seminar.

In 1933, the local government around both Neuchatel and Geneva became "obsessively anticommunist" (Vidal, 1989, p. 103). The resulting political pressures, by 1922, tied Piaget's Jean-Jacques Rousseau Institute's funding to reorganization. Its original "red pedagogy" (Vidal, 1989, p. 103) required elimination. Piaget was part of that change. The change also enabled Piaget to push his ideas forward. "Thus, the political circumstances that neutralized the Rousseau Institute also furthered Piaget's career and were consistent with the relinquishing of his moral enterprise" (Vidal, 1989, p. 104). Piaget would go on to become a professor emeritus, head of the United Nations International Bureau of Education, and a renowned author.

Vygotsky

Vygotsky quickly moved from being an assistant researcher to a department head at the Kornilov Institute. Lenin did not get total control of the USSR until 1922 but died in 1924. When Stalin made his bid for complete dictatorship, one of the first to die was Vygotsky's mentor and boss, Kornilov. His execution in 1929 made Vygotsky flee Moscow. Vygotsky was to live and do research in Ukraine, Central Asia, and Uzbekistan. There, Vygotsky finished the medical degree that he had begun at the Imperial Moscow University but had dropped in favor of law—although he never practiced medicine (Ratner, 1991). This may be because, in 1934, Stalin ordered him to stand trial for "political error." Vygotsky died at Serebryany Bor Sanatorium on June 11, 1934, while working on his defense. He was only 38 years old. Stalin had Vygotsky's work repressed for over 20 years. Stalin died in 1953. The publications of Vygotsky's works resumed in 1956. In all, he produced 180 works but most of these did not reach the West until Gorbachev's administration.

Although both were often concerned with the negative aspects of human behavior, neither illnesses nor Stalin's repression could stop their freedom-loving spirits. They most certainly heard of each other's work early in their respective careers and tried repeatedly but sometimes furtively to communicate those ideas with each other. In view of the differences in their countries, religions, careers, and personalities, they could easily have become rivals and critics of each other. But, in reality, both Piaget and Vygotsky respected each other's ideas. Stymied in such endeavors by Stalin's desire to cut off all east–west communications, the two men, nevertheless, did manage to influence each other to a limited extent.

CHAPTER 5

ORIGIN OF IDEAS

INTRODUCTION

The lives, problems, work, and efforts of both Piaget and Vygotsky came together to delineate two pedagogies that contained an epistemology (the study of thinking). These men did not create their works in a vacuum.

The following six factors influence all human thought and actions: political/military, economic, science, social, philosophy, religion, and art/education. This premise is based on an analytical tool first developed by Professor Harold Quigley of Georgetown University's School of Foreign Service in 1944. Quigley's Curve is still used today by the departments of state and defense to predict international crises' outcomes. This curve (Chart 2) also adapts to reveal the germinal image. The germinal image is the origin of a creative work (Andres, 1998). It is an emotional experience so intense that the individual is compelled to create (Andres, 1988).

For both countries and individuals, this germinal image can be to create either a civilization or a concept. For both Piaget and Vygotsky, their germinal image is found in the optimal mismatch that arose within them when facing their respective difficulties. For Piaget, it arose because of a dysfunctional family. For Vygotsky, it arose because of a dysfunctional country.

For genetic epistemology, Quigley's Curve traces the origins of equilibration, chronological stages of development, role of language, teacher as diagnostician, error, independence of the learner, optimal mismatch, and play. For cultural–historical theory, the curve traces the origins of zone of proximal development (ZPD), internalization, stages of development, the

Parallel Paths to Constructivism: Jean Piaget and Lev Vygotsky, pages 57–93

"social other," role of communication, error, sociohistorical context of learning, scaffolding, and play. For the sake of explanation and clarification, some facts already presented will be repeated in this chapter.

HUMANITY AND THE CURVE

All humans go through five stages of life, namely, birth, development, maturity, seniority, and death. Sometimes, as in the case of wars or epidemics, humans can move through these stages very rapidly. Sometimes, if one has a lingering illness, one can move through the stages rather slowly. Maturity is relative to the age of the person when they died. For example, not all people live to see middle age. Nevertheless, the goal of most humans is to enter senior citizenship before death. While Vygotsky died when he was 38, Piaget lived until he was 80.

THE CURVE IN BIOGRAPHICAL ANALYSIS

Countries are made up of people and the overriding factor in the demise of civilizations, according to Quigley, is the amount of self-centeredness in the majority of the people. Adapted to humans, Quigley's Curve is able to analyze not only a person's chronological stages of development but also their ideas. This study presents the argument that an adaptation of Quigley's Curve can be used to trace the motivations of both Piaget and Vygotsky in creating their respective theories. Quigley's Curve can also be used to trace the origin of the ideas enclosed within those respective theories.

Just like the comparative biography of this study showed the similarities between the personal lives of Piaget and Vygotsky, the analysis section of this study will show the similarities within the origins of their respective ideas. Because some people who affected Piaget and Vygotsky are subject to analysis within more than one factor due to the scope of their contributions, there will be some overlap. For example, the influence of Dr. Henri Pieron is found within both the economic (as an employer) and science/technology (providing psychology as a link between science and epistemology) factors.

This analysis also indicated the adversity that each man faced. There is no creativity without adversity (John-Steiner, 1985). Where and when you live engenders your identity (R. Hamilton, personal communication). Other people besides Piaget and Vygotsky have encountered such a milieu. Therefore, I believe that what Piaget and Vygotsky did to overcome adversity can be taught to others. For example, a solution that both Piaget and Vygotsky accomplished was to become intellectually creative. How they did so might help teachers develop creativity within their own students.

POLITICAL/MILITARY

The lives and ideas of Piaget and Vygotsky were most opposite when seen in the light of their respective country's government and involvement in wars. Both lived during World War I. Both lived during the start and spread of communism. Both lived during Stalin's reign of terror when all communication between the USSR and Europe was cut off. However, because his country was a democracy that did not fight during the turbulent 20th century, the war had less impact on Piaget.

Piaget

Piaget's peaceful, democratic Switzerland, which was neutral in time of war, provided a more stable, less stressful environment. Nevertheless, World War I did affect Piaget's psyche. Piaget helped his mother as she volunteered assistance to prisoners of war from both sides of the conflict. What Piaget saw encouraged him to reject organized, established religion (Piaget, 1952). I believe that, if this had not happened, Piaget would not have turned to philosophy—the heart of which is epistemology. After that, Piaget strove to reconcile science and religion by purging philosophy of its irrational subjectivity (Montangero & Maurice-Naville, 1997). In demographically and ideologically homogeneous Switzerland, individualism and freedom were preserved and encouraged. Because of this, Piaget felt comfortable concentrating on how an individual learns, rather than how the group influences.

Vygotsky

Vygotsky, on the other hand, endured first, autocratic Czarist repression; second, World War I; third, the Russian Revolution and Leninism; and finally, Stalin's dictatorship and purges. I believe that, if the Russian government had been less prejudiced, Vygotsky would not have invented cultural–historical theory. While still a child, Vygotsky experienced anti-Jewish pogroms in 1903 (Pinkus, 1988) and 1906 (Gilbert, 1979). He also experienced watching his father being put on trial for organizing a successful defense of Gomel (Blanck, 1990). Although acquitted, Vygotsky's father became "embittered" (van der Veer & Valsiner, 1991, p. 5) by Czarist persecutions. Vygotsky, himself, would later write on anti-Semitism (Vygotsky, 1916). These problems would cause Vygotsky to develop a deep sense of fatalism and become interested in literary pathos (van der Veer & Valsiner, 1991) and, eventually, defending Leninism (Rissom, 1985).

While neither man fought in World War I, it impacted both. The conflict, however, impacted Vygotsky more than it did Piaget. Besides bringing about the Russian Revolution, World War I also deprived Vygotsky and his family of adequate food and fuel. The result was that both Vygotsky and his favorite brother, Dodik, would contract tuberculosis that both would eventually die from. Dodik died during the Russian Revolution and his death made Vygotsky's psyche deteriorate into a deeper nervous tension (Blanck, 1990). The treatment for tuberculosis back then was plenty of rest at a sanitarium. Vygotsky would have plenty of time to think and reflect during his multiple hospitalizations, until his death in 1934.

Time for individual reflection is needed in all creative endeavors. During hospitalization for a 1924 attack, Vygotsky finished *The Psychology of Art*, his dissertation thesis. In 1925, still confined to the sanitarium, he wrote *The Historical Meaning of the Crisis in Psychology*. He was hospitalized again in 1933. From his deathbed at the sanitarium in 1934, he dictated the last chapter of *Thinking and Speech*, which is said to be, "In my opinion, one of the most beautiful pieces of psychological literature of all time" (Blanck, 1990).

Piaget came to see communism differently. Despite his mother being a Christian socialist, Piaget saw communist repression (especially under Stalin) as particularly negative—so much so that, during part of his professional career, he would reject some of Vygotsky's ideas as examples of what a Stalinist dictatorship could use to imprison young minds.

Without the Russian Revolution, Vygotsky would not have become trapped in Kiev. If that had not happened, and if Lenin had not opened up public teaching to Jews, Vygotsky would never have researched cultural—historical theory

It was a combination of attacks by the White Army, a history of Czarist repression, and the fact that Lenin would not allow anti-Semitism in his USSR that made Vygotsky see Leninism as liberating and he wanted to make sure that "Marxist–Leninist principles would succeed" (Wertsch, 1985, p. 10). So, without World War I and the Russian Revolution, Vygotsky's cultural–historical theory would never have been written because he would have never received the opportunity to do so.

Conclusion

Despite living in countries with completely opposite governments and histories, the political and military pillars of their nations did impact both Piaget and Vygotsky to create their respective pedagogies in an attempt to prevent similar unhappiness from impacting others. Indeed, one may ask what would Vygotsky have created if he was raised in democratic, peaceful

Switzerland and what would Piaget have created if he had been born in Czarist Russia with all the tragedy endured by its people in this century?

ECONOMIC

"Middle class" is both an economic and social label. Revolutions are middle-class movements. Both Piaget and Vygotsky were middle class and revolutionary. Their pedagogies revolutionized education. Because both their hometowns and families were middle class, both Piaget and Vygotsky were products of middle-class environments. The middle-class morality adhered to by both encouraged intellectual pursuits and academic endeavors. Both sets of parents were supporters of their town's culture. Piaget's father wrote a book about the town's history and his mother worked for humane treatment of POWs from both sides of the war. Vygotsky's parents started their town's library. They also supported many cultural activities for Gomel, such as literary debating societies and plays.

Swiss prosperity continued despite world wars and the Great Depression. Piaget's students enjoyed all that was necessary for a rich, inquiring, academic environment. Thus, Piaget could afford to have students taught in an educationally rich environment correctly set to their stage of development. Vygotsky could not. The people of the USSR faced severe economic depression during World War I, during the Russian Revolution, and during the 1930s. Thus, Vygotsky chose to use a cheaper "social other" rather than an inquiry-rich environment to format his ideas. However, both men, raised in middle-class families, received the best education that their families and countries could provide. This made education important to both Piaget and Vygotsky.

The final part of the economic factor is employment. The learning and ideas for both men came to fruition during their postgraduate employment. It was their on-the-job activities during their first employment after getting their baccalaureate that allowed both men to begin preliminary research on all the ideas that their life experiences gave them. This research, based on all that they had learned, proved their ideas correct.

Piaget

Piaget had a "job" when he was still a youth. Piaget learned about chronological stages of development, assimilation, and equilibration from his job at the well-endowed Neuchatel Museum of Natural History under the tutelage of Paul Godet (Piaget, 1952, 1966a, 1976) while watching specimens in the museum's laboratory (Isaaca, 1974; Pieron, 1966). He was paid in specimens (i.e., mollusks and snails), which he collected and catalogued. Piaget's observations, this collection, and the reading of Herbert Spencer and Charles Darwin, suggested that Piaget could apply the evolutionist approach to studying the psychology of knowledge (Piaget, 1952; Spencer, 1855).

Piaget's employment after a semester studying psychology at the University of Zurich also influenced him. In Paris, Piaget worked with Dr. Theodore Simon, Dr. Pierre Janet, and Dr. Henri Pieron developing an intelligence test in Dr. Alfred Binet's laboratories. Dr. Simon and Dr. Binet divided children's development into stages (Binet & Simon, 1905). This endorsed what Piaget learned while a child at the Neuchatel Museum of Natural History. Dr. Pierre Janet worked on a genetic approach to the psychology of behavior. He also formulated ideas about the hierarchical organization of psychological functions (Amman-Gainotti, 1992). These ideas also confirmed Piaget's childhood observations.

However, while working at a new job in the rue de la Grange aux Belles, Piaget became more interested in why children fail to learn. Offered Dr. Binet's well-equipped laboratory, Piaget started research there to prove his earlier pedagogical ideas correct. "What had been at the outset nothing but a boring and annoying situation became a real dialogue with suggestions" (Gruber & Vonche, 1995, p. 53). A new method of interrogating children was born. Piaget used this method to lead the child to show how he formulates, solves, and thinks. From Dr. Simon and Dr. Pieron, Piaget became interested in child psychology. However, it was while working directly for Dr. Janet that Piaget observed the notion of intelligence as an adaptation to new circumstances. Later, at the Jean-Jacques Rousseau Institute, Piaget observed that his boss and former mentor, Edouard Claparede, Director of the Jean-Jacques Rousseau Institute in Geneva, accepted Janet's idea. It was Claparede who started the so-called "activity schools" in which a child investigated educational challenges that were appropriate for that child's chronological stage of development while in an academically rich learning environment (N. Colet, personal communication, March 15, 1999). Claparede allowed Piaget free observational research, as long as Piaget studied cognitive learning and this exactly matched Piaget's new interest that began during his postgraduate work in Paris.

In Paris, Piaget observed children only in the hospital. However, in Geneva working at the Jean-Jacques Rousseau Institute, Piaget observed children in more natural surroundings, such as the school, la maison des petits (Munari, 1994). This created an interest in pedagogy. Claparede defined intelligence as adaptation whose function was to compensate for the deficiencies of innate or automated adaptations. Claparede also showed the biological foundation of mental activity and gave Piaget a functional explanation of behavior (Montangero & Maurice-Naville, 1997).

Vygotsky

Vygotsky returned from Kiev to Gomel only to discover that his world had changed. Unlike under the czars, he was no longer restricted to teaching in just Jewish schools (Blanck, 1990). Vygotsky started working many jobs at once and they were all in the field of education. For the next 7 years, he taught literature and Russian at the local Labor School. He also taught classes on aesthetics and the history of art at a local conservatory (Wertsch, 1985). He built a psychology laboratory at the Gomel Teachers' College, where he delivered a series of lectures that provided the groundwork for one of his first major books, *Pedagogical Psychology* (van der Veer & Valsiner, 1991; Wertsch, 1985). This is not the only testament to Vygotsky's growing pedagogical interest. He taught courses in logic and psychology at the Pedagogical Institute. In addition, he worked teaching literature and education courses at the Workers' Faculty and adult schools, including technical schools for pressmen and metallurgists (G. Vygodskaya, personal communication, 1984). Vygotsky also headed the theater section of the Gomel Department of People's Education, cooperating with one of its organizers, Ilya Danjushevsky, who would later invite him to Moscow to work in the field of defectology.

In these cases, it was the state or USSR government that was functioning as the "social other." When Vygotsky did independent work, like Piaget enjoyed, he failed. Vygotsky edited and published articles in the theater section of a local newspaper. He also started a publishing venture called "Ages and Days," which printed only two literary works: *Fire*, a collection of poems of Ilya Erhenburg, and a collection of poems by Jean Moreas (Dobkin, 1982). He was one of the founders of a literary magazine entitled *Veresk*. If these had not failed, Vygotsky probably would have been a successful editor and not bothered to go into educational psychology.

Vygotsky also did volunteer work. He was at the center of Gomel's intellectual avant garde. He started Literary Mondays, where his friends and neighbors discussed new prose and poetry. Later, some could still recall his lectures on Shakespeare, Chekhov, Pushing, Einstein, and the theory of relativity (G. Vygodskaya, personal communication, 1984). Now, educational psychology had become his central concern (Blanck, 1990) but his experiences made him focus on the social rather than individual aspects of pedagogy and realize that language could be a tool of learning.

Conclusion

All revolutions are middle class. Both Piaget and Vygotsky created revolutions in pedagogy. Without their middle-class backgrounds, they would not have done so. If born rich, they would have been members of the establishment and, therefore, not prone to reform. If born poor, they might not have received the education necessary to launch them into their careers.

SCIENCE

Since psychology is a science, the leading psychologists of their day influenced both Vygotsky and Piaget who would also influence each other. Gestalt psychology taught that one couldn't break up perception into its various parts and study those parts separately. The human psyche demands that perception (seeing, hearing, feeling) is observable as a whole. That observance points out intellectual patterns. Gestalt psychology, thus, was a Hegelian antithesis to empiricism and behaviorism. Piaget and Vygotsky created their learning theories partially in order to combat the Gestaltists. They also created their theories to combat the empiricists and behavioralists. The empiricists were too irrational with their introspective approach to theory (Piaget, 1952) and the behaviorists ignored human consciousness or free will (Vygotsky, 1924).

The works of biologist Charles Darwin and psychologist/philosopher Herbert Spencer also influenced both Piaget and Vygotsky. Vygotsky would build upon their theories of evolution to prove Marxism correct by providing a cultural–historical context for learning. Piaget would react using their idea to create a biological explanation for the evolution of human learning.

Piaget

After receiving his doctorate in 1918 with a dissertation on the mollusks of Valais (Piaget, 1921), Piaget traveled to Zurich for postgraduate study and work. There, he visited Lipps's and Wreschner's psychological laboratories and Bleuler's psychiatric clinic. He "felt at once that there lay my path...in utilizing for psychological experimentation, the mental habits I had acquired in zoology" (Piaget, 1952, p. 243). The contact with Bleuler was a lasting influence because it brought Piaget again into contact with the theories of Freud and Jung (Chapman, 1988). As Piaget investigated these theories, he was to personally reject them because of their irrational nature (Piaget, 1952, 1966a, 1976). In fact, Piaget saw genetic epistemology as an effort to purify psychology from such irrational influences (Piaget, 1952, 1976).

In the fall of 1919, Piaget attended lectures on the philosophy of science by L. Brunschvicg, whose psychological orientation and historical–critical method would exert a lasting influence on him, as attested to by the many references to Brunschvicg in Piaget's writings on the epistemology of science (Chapman, 1988). However, it was Piaget's encounter with Dr. Theodore Simon that first steered Piaget toward educational psychology, especially with the use of the Dr. Binet's laboratory. As explained earlier, this was made available to Piaget by Dr. Simon on the death of his partner (Binet), as Dr. Simon could not use it because he was living in Rouen.

There were three psychologists who influenced Piaget as he worked on testing intelligence: Dr. Cyril Burt, Dr. Henri Pieron, and Dr. Pierre Janet. With the death of Binet, the project needed a young, inquiring mind that could do independent work. So, Janet hired Piaget for the purpose of standardizing Dr. Burt's test of reasoning on Paris schoolchildren at the Ecole de la rue de la Grange-aux-Belles. However, Piaget wrote, "I never really did it. Standardization was not at all interesting; I preferred to work with the errors on the test" (Hall, 1970, p. 27). I believe that Piaget thought that, if he could discover the reason for inaccurate reasoning, he might be able to discover the reason for his mother's mental illness and his own two nervous breakdowns. Piaget's mentor, Pierre Janet (also at odds with Freud), allowed Piaget free rein, Piaget was able to use this time to study psychoanalytic techniques. These and other clinical observations in Binet's laboratory were to form the background for Piaget's psychological research and would directly lead to the creation of genetic epistemology.

Until he arrived in Paris for his postgraduate work, Piaget had possessed only a very general theoretical system and a desire for experimentation. He also lacked a concrete area of investigation. By assimilating Burt's methods to his own preexisting notion of structure, Piaget transformed the task that Simon had set for him into something different; namely, failures in learning (Chapman, 1988; Piaget, 1952). Dr. Pieron also worked on the following topics that influenced Piaget to create genetic epistemology, namely, evolution of the psyche, relationships between human and animal learning, and the structure of memory (Pieron, 1929).

Pieron established the field of psychophysiology. He provided the link Piaget needed between earlier zoological studies and an evolution of thinking. Dr. Janet investigated hierarchical levels of behavior (Janet, 1926). He had three stages and directly influenced Piaget to think about the evolution of epistemology. Piaget used these periods but he made some changes: he divided them into four stages and divided them chronologically. Piaget's stages are sensorimotor (birth until 1½ years), concrete operations (1½ years until 8 years), and formal operations (8 years onward).

The first psychologists to have considered mental development as passing through a series of steps or stages were Wilhelm Preyer (1882) and James Baldwin (1894). Both Janet and Piaget read these authors and conversed on their ideas. Janet was the first to describe feelings by regulations of action

(Janet, 1902). Janet was also the first, however, to set stages whose periods of development influenced Piaget's chronological stages of development. Janet obtained this concept from the 18th-century concept of regulation used in economics and physiology (Montangero & Maurice-Naville, 1997).

Building on this, a fourth psychologist, Edouarde Claparede, defined mental life and all living organisms by their self-regulating ability, which allowed a return to equilibrium each time this was lost (Claparede, 1917). Claparede recalled the parallel between this idea and Le Chatelier's law of thermodynamic equilibrium in physical chemistry, to which Piaget often referred (Montangero & Maurice-Naville, 1997). Piaget's concept of sel-regulation was born.

The philosopher Henri Bergson inspired two American psychologists (William James and James Baldwin) to write on the notions of evolution and tie this to the field of psychology. Piaget was influenced by the functionalism of James (1909) and the genetic approach of Baldwin (1894). However, it was Claparede who tied their work together for Piaget. Claparede "had the most direct influence of Piaget's thinking, for he showed the biological foundation of mental activity and gave a functional explanation of behavior" (Montangero & Maurice-Naville, 1997, p. 71).

In his 1952 and 1976 autobiographies, Piaget described how, as an adolescent, he was interested in two fields of inquiry: natural science and the philosophy of knowledge. These two modes of inquiry were to lay the foundation for his later work. Again, Charles Darwin impacted both fields dynamically during Piaget's formative years. Some researchers believe that Piaget created genetic epistemology to trace the evolution of human learning (B. Peterman, personal communication, October 20, 1996). However, biologists other than Charles Darwin also made an impact on Piaget.

Piaget was greatly influenced by French-speaking biologists "who, although recognizing the importance of interaction with the environment, did not refute the Darwinian idea of natural selection" (Montangero & Maurice-Naville, 1997, p. 3). Piaget found concepts in Le Dantec's works that he later adapted and adopted himself, such as equilibrium, assimilation, and imitation (Le Dantec, 1895). Evolutionary biologist Charles Darwin and evolutionary philosopher Herbert Spencer influenced Piaget. Darwin and Spencer also influenced other writers such as Bergson, Sabatier, Baldwin, and Reymond, whose works both Piaget and Vygotsky read. It was by reading an 1896 work of Henry Bergson that "Piaget discovered the idea that biological evolution creates increasingly complex forms, which are extended on the intellectual level" (Montangero & Maurice-Naville, 1997, p. 70). This book by Bergson influenced Piaget's plan to develop a biological theory of knowledge (Peterman, 1997). From Baldwin, "Piaget borrowed the notion of accommodation, who had borrowed it from Spencer" (Montangero & Maurice-Naville, 1997, p. 66).

Vygotsky

While science impacted Piaget's thinking, it was the humanities that influenced Vygotsky. Vygotsky used his knowledge of philosophy, history, philology, and literary analysis to combat what he believed was wrong with science (psychology) with his cultural–historical theory. Vygotsky's 1924 paper, entitled *The Methodology of Reflexology and Psychological Studies*, was a thinly veiled criticism of both Pavlov and Bekhterev (The Vygotsky Group, 1996). Vygotsky claimed in this paper that the behaviorists "cannot ignore the facts of consciousness" (The Vygotsky Group, 1996). Quoting from the work of both Pavlov and Bekhterev, Vygotsky showed that both researchers acknowledged the important role of "subjective experience" or consciousness in daily life, but "deemed the scientific study of this role impossible" (van der Veer & Valsiner, p. 41). Vygotsky disagreed with them.

Besides his famous *Methodology of Reflexology and Psychological Studies* address, Vygotsky also read two other papers at the Second Psychoneurological Congress in Leningrad. One was entitled *How We Have to Teach Psychology Now*. The other one, presented a few days later, was entitled *The Results of a Survey on the Mood of Pupils in the Final Classes of the Gomel Schools in 1923* (G. Vygodskaya, personal communication, April 5, 1989). Vygotsky demonstrated his desire as a psychologist to reform this discipline with these papers.

After listening to Vygotsky deliver his paper that attacked the behaviorists, A.R. Luria, the academic secretary at the Moscow Institute of Psychology, asked (along with Lenin's wife and the USSR's Director of Education) its director, K.N. Kornilov, to invite Vygotsky to Moscow (Luria, 1976). Kornilov stressed the developmental nature of all intellectual processes (Kornilov, 1922). This encouraged Vygotsky to start creating a concept that he had effectively experimented with in Gomel. Upon arriving in Moscow, Vygotsky quickly set up a troika of psychologists with Luria and Leont'ev to create cultural–historical theory (van der Veer & Valsiner, 1991).

In the late 1920s, Vygotsky, while working to finish the medical degree he had begun at the University of Moscow in 1913 (Rissom, 1985), became interested in the work of Kurt Goldstein. Goldstein believed in a holistic perspective to neurology (Goldstein & Gelb, 1920). Goldstein's work provided an endorsement for Vygotsky's ideas on thought and communication (Goldstein, 1948). Goldstein, working in defectology, reported that patients sometimes lacked the capability to follow abstract instructions. This supported Vygotsky's views on the role of concepts in organizing a person's thought processes (Vygotsky, letter to Levina, July 16, 1931).

Later, Vygotsky would try to communicate with other Western psychologists such as Piaget, Meumann, and Montessori. However, Stalin's dictatorship effectively cut off such attempts at east–west communication by 1929.

Before that happened, Piaget contributed to Vygotsky the idea of stages of epistemological development in humans (Vygotsky, 1926) and Meumann confirmed the strong role of the intellect in human psychology or the "so-called activity theory" (Leontiev, 1975). Montessori confirmed what Vygotsky's classroom experiences in Gomel had taught him about childhood learning (Vygotsky, letter to Leontiev, July 11, 1929). In addition, the American psychologist Dorothea McCardle contributed the name (but not the idea) of zone of proximal development (Kozyrev & Turko, 1935).

Conclusion

If it had not been for flexibility within their respective nation's scientific environments, neither Piaget nor Vygotsky could have created their learning theories. Instead, Piaget would have been a natural scientist and Vygotsky would have been a literary critic and/or teacher.

In addition, as they continued their further inquires, each man was influenced by the leading psychologists of his day and saw that psychology could be improved. Despite this, both men rejected the major psychological schools of their time (e.g., Gestalt, behavioralism, and empiricism) and decided to embark on independent work. However, the greatest influence that moved them to create these came not from science, but from their respective social milieus.

SOCIAL

Both Neuchatel and Gomel were medium-size, bourgeoisie towns that were the intellectual center of their areas. If the parents could not help a child, both communities had people within them that would (and did) help that child. Both towns remembered persecutions, and that made them even more close-knit and more nurturing than normal small towns tend to be.

Both sets of parents also contributed to the culture of their respective towns. Piaget's father wrote a history of Neuchatel and was a respected professor of medieval literature at the local university. Some of his colleagues and friends became Piaget's mentors (like Arnold Reymond). Piaget's mother was elected to the local school board and was active in obtaining humane treatment for prisoners of war on both sides of World War I (Newman & Holzman, 1993). Vygotsky's parents established Gomel's library. Vygotsky's father, Semyon, was an executive of the United Bank of Gomel who defended that town effectively during a czarist pogrom and, thus, saved many lives. His mother, Cecilia, encouraged literary and philosophical discussion groups with friends and neighbors (Blanck, 1990). Together, Vygotsky's parents set up zones of proximal development (ZPD) all over town—an example that Vygotsky would copy many times over. In these ZPDs, the parents took turns being the "social other" to guide their children intellectually and deepen their knowledge and understanding of philosophy and literary analysis.

Both fathers were similar in personality. Both fathers enjoyed reading philosophy and introduced their sons to Kant and Hegel, whose philosophies were useful for the creation of both genetic epistemology and cultural–historical theory. The fathers served as models for their sons. Both fathers were hard workers and successful within their fields. Both fathers, however, had a negative side to their personality that the sons adopted.

Arthur Piaget was "a man of painstaking and critical mind, who disliked hastily improved generalizations" but who also taught his son "the value of systematic work, even in small matters " (Piaget, 1952, p. 237). Piaget says that he got his "love of facts" from his father, who advised his son not to study in the humanities because "it wasn't a true science" (Piaget, 1976, p. 7). So, Piaget would endeavor to make it a true science with genetic epistemology.

Semyon Vygodsky had "a rather stern disposition and bitter ironic humor " (Wertsch, 1985, p. 3). The persecutions and pogroms that Russian Jews suffered developed a deep bitterness within Semyon that developed into a deep fatalism in his son (Blanck, 1990). Thus, from childhood, Vygotsky had a predilection for literary tragedy and pathos (Vygodskaya & Lifanova, 1996) and this encouraged him to focus on literary analysis, from which he got the idea of the importance of language.

The similarities between Piaget's and Vygotsky's social biographies end with the comparisons of their hometowns and their fathers. The only similarities between both men's mothers were that both were intelligent and both influenced their sons to help others. Otherwise, they were very different. Vygotsky was close to his seven siblings and also to most of his cousins. Together with his young relatives, he set up ZPDs with them. Here, the children took turns teaching and learning from each other as they put on plays, held debates, and analyzed literature.

Piaget was not close to his two sisters. Since Fernando Vidal's 1994 book, *Piaget Before Piaget*, Piaget's family has refused all interviews. Vidal quoted Piaget's oldest sister, Rebecca-Suzanne, as describing their mother as "neurotic" (Vidal, 1994, p. 14). Vidal also quoted Piaget's other sister as saying that the mother was "an authoritarian woman who made their childhood unhappy" (Vidal, 1994, p. 14). She was hospitalized for 3 months for persecution psychosis. Upon release, she antagonized the Swiss Red Cross by incorrectly charging them with mistreatment of German prisoners of war. She only won acquittal in court because she made general charges and did not name any names (Vidal, 1994).

Vygotsky had many "social others": close family, good friends, and effective teachers who also functioned as effective mentors. So, Vygotsky would develop the idea that learning takes place via a "social other." Piaget had a dysfunctional family, no close friends, and all his teachers did him more harm than good (Piaget, 1932). So, Piaget would write of the independence of the learner because that is how he learned.

Piaget

Starting with his 1952 autobiography, Piaget revealed much about his unhappy family life in childhood. His mother's "neurotic temperament" made "our family life somewhat troublesome" (Piaget, 1952, p. 237). His father, Arthur Piaget, was cold, distant, and critical. To escape this unhappy situation with Rebecca Piaget, the father retired into solitary study of medieval literature and the son abandoned play for serious work "very early. . .as much to imitate my father as to take refuge in a. . .nonficticious world" (p. 238). The success that Piaget consequently had as a solitary learner laid the foundation for his ideas of teacher as diagnostician and independence of the learner.

In his 1976 autobiography, Piaget wrote that he became interested in psychology as much as a method to find a reason or cure for his mother's mental illness as a field of study. His mother created two crises in his life. The first one was theological and the second one was philosophical (Piaget, 1952, 1976). Out of these two crises came the ideas of accommodation, assimilation, and equilibration (Piaget, 1980).

Piaget would reject Vygotsky's idea of the "social other" because, in addition to his parents, anyone placed by society in that position for him, failed him. Unlike Vygotsky, Piaget never had a close relationship with people his own age until after he started his professional career. Those who helped him were older people who helped him because they wanted to, not because they were directly employed in a social role to do so. The mentoring by older people (who correctly diagnosed the problems of Piaget and solutions to those problems) effectively directed Piaget's work; so, Piaget created the role of the teacher to be more diagnostician than active educator in the classroom.

This was especially true in Paris, where Piaget functioned as a diagnostician, a role that his earlier mentors played for him. Because he observed that this worked for the students he was diagnosing in Paris, Piaget would emphasize the independence of the learner and the teacher as diagnostician in his written works. Piaget was never employed as a teacher.

Because his childhood was so unhappy, Piaget set about building an epistemology to prevent this happening to other children. Helping him to do this were three Neuchatel clubs: the Friends of Nature, the Jura Club, and the Association of Christian-Swiss Students. The first two clubs encouraged Piaget in his zoological studies and confirmed his idea of chronological stages of development. The third club provided him with a foundation upon which he would explore (but later reject) formal theology in favor of philosophy.

Because of his mother, a Christian socialist, and the Association of Christian-Swiss Students, Piaget was briefly a socialist. Unlike Vygotsky, the writings of Karl Marx had little influence on Piaget. Like Vygotsky, he was caught up in the bandwagon flurry of activity after the Communist Revolution. It looked as if good reforms were about to take place. It was not until after Lenin died and Stalin started his repression that Piaget would reject any form of socialism. Stalin's authoritative dictatorship and accompanying purges had a lot to do with Piaget rejecting some of Vygotsky's most important ideas; namely, the "social other" and the dialectics of language. I believe this was done because Piaget thought Vygotsky's approach could empower a Stalinist-type government to have power over the minds of children.

Vygotsky

Lev Vygotsky changed his name from Vygodskya to Vygotsky while in his early 20s "because he believed—after some research of his own—that his family originally came from a village called Vygotovo. No one has been able to establish its location"; so, his two daughters returned to the original family name of Vygodskaya (van der Veer & Valsiner, 1991, p. 4). Vygotsky was the second child in a family of eight children (including him). When he was about a year old, his family moved from Orsha, where he was born, to Gomel, a somewhat larger town that was also in Belorussia. It was here that Vygotsky spent his childhood and youth.

From his father, Vygotsky obtained the idea that both the teacher and the student need intellectual freedom. However, because of what his father went through with Czarist pogroms and because of his subsequent bitterness, Vygotsky also received the idea that life is a constant struggle that ends in death. Vygotsky would extend these ideas of freedom and fatalism into his research and work.

Vygotsky's father led the cultural activities in Gomel. He and his wife established the local public library, whose books Vygotsky "avidly devoured" (Yaroshevski, 1996, p. 330). The couple provided a warm, intellectually stimulating atmosphere for their children. This influenced Vygotsky to concentrate on the importance of the "social other" but also to insist that the "social other" encourage free thinking. In the evenings, Vygotsky's father and mother would hold cultural sessions in the dining room around the samovar. "These conversations would play a decisive role in the children's cultural formation" (Blanck, 1990, p. 32). When the children became older, their parents encouraged them during these meetings to either refute or endorse the ideas of Spinoza, Hegel, Nietzsche, Spencer, and Tyler. The father's study was always open to the family, a habit Vygotsky would later continue with his own family. Vygotsky, his siblings, and his friends would enjoy playing and studying there (Vygodskaya, 1994/1996). The territorial restrictions, strict quotas for entrance to the university, prohibition from many professions, and permanent threat of a pogrom contributed to the closeness of the family and community of Gomel (Blanck, 1990).

Vygotsky's mother, Cecilia Moiseievna, was a licensed teacher who resigned to devote all her time to taking care of her family and home. From his mother, Lev Vygotsky received his initial knowledge of German (G. Vygodskaya, 1981, in Wertsch, 1985). She also introduced him to the poet Heine and the philosopher Spinoza (Blanck, 1990). From his mother, Vygotsky picked up a love of literature, poetry, and drama. He preferred, however, tragedies. This came from his father's bitterness and his country's repression (Dobkin, 1982). Pushkin's tragic works would become Vygotsky's "favorite" literature (Blanck, 1990, p. 33). He also enjoyed analyzing *Hamlet*. It was from his mother that Vygotsky began his love of literature and its analysis.

Building on this love of language and literature, Vygotsky would hold discussion groups with his sister Zinaida, cousin David, and brother Dodik. Zinaida was to become a prominent linguist and coauthor of several foreign language dictionaries. His sister, cousin, brother, and friend (Semyon Dobkin) would encourage Vygotsky to see the importance of language.

Language was important to Vygotsky. He read Hebrew, Latin, Greek, French, German, and English. Vygotsky, however, refused to speak nonnative languages because his pronunciation "did not live up to his own high standards" (Vygodskaya, in Wertsch, 1985, p. 233) Starting in 1920, he would build upon the linguistic ideas that his sister, Zinaida, gave him to argue that children originally use speech for social reasons, although they eventually internalize language as well. This new internalization, Vygotsky would later call "inner speech." Vygotsky believed that inner speech made thought processes more efficient and abstract than they were before (van der Veer & Valsiner, 1991, p. 559).

Conclusion

Considering all the factors that influenced Piaget and Vygotsky, the social factor had the greatest influence on both men. Without the influence that their hometowns, parents, siblings, friends, mentors, and teachers had on them, Piaget and Vygotsky would never have created their respective pedagogies.

Piaget's family (with its adversity) caused him to believe in solitary inquiry of the learner while still a child. His lack of close childhood friends his own age and his lack of closeness to his sisters or classroom teachers made him reject a "social other" as an instructor early in life. Vygotsky, on the other hand, began in early childhood to believe in the "social other" and communication as a teaching tool because his family, friends, siblings, teachers, and mentors were close to him and very helpful. It was within this social factor that both men encountered philosophy, and that was to have an impact on their work.

PHILOSOPHY

The fathers of both Piaget and Vygotsky introduced their sons to philosophy, namely, Kant and Hegel. Both fathers and sons accepted Kant's union of empiricism and rationalism by use of the scientific method. Both also accepted Kant's theory that man can determine his own history. Kant presumed that all knowledge enters as perception and all knowledge begins in experience. However, one must introspect on this and one must shape perception by the structure of one's consciousness (T. Schaeffer, personal communication, June 18, 1998). Both Piaget and Vygotsky believed Kant when he postulated that man can find reason via the will, that man can become his own god, and duty exists for its own sake. These ideas formed the basis for the life work of both men.

Both Piaget and Vygotsky used Hegel's dialectics of thesis, antithesis, and synthesis in their ideas. Hegel also wrote that man's reason is in constant flux (Montangero & Maurice-Naville, 1997). Piaget used Hegel's philosophy to explain the process of perception, assimilation, and equilibration. Vygotsky used it to explain how communication and the sociohistorical march of knowledge prove Marx and Engle's dialectical materialism correct.

Piaget

Piaget's *The Mission of the Idea* (1915) and *Recherche* (1918/1980) show the influence of socialism upon him. However, it was more from his mother's influence than that of Karl Marx that Piaget became a socialist. When Stalin began his terrible dictatorship with its many purges, Piaget was to forego socialism all together, but not before he rejected established Christianity in favor of philosophy.

The philosopher Henri Bergson had a large impact on Piaget and was the direct cause of Piaget's first novel, *Reschere*. Henri Bergson was a French anti-intellectual philosopher. Piaget (1952) wrote that Bergson's parts-in-the-whole schema created a bridge in Piaget's mind between science and philosophy. Bergson's idea of creative evolution laid the foundation for Piaget's genetic epistemology because it was Bergson that wrote the intellect secures a perfect fit to the environment "by a process of adaptation" (Balestra, 1980, p. 416). Piaget would later elaborate on the details of this adaptation to form the idea of equilibration. Bergson's idea that biological transformations led to the birth and process of intelligence formed the basis of Piaget's stages of development (Balestra, 1980).

While searching for a way to avoid a dualistic theory of knowledge, Piaget was influenced by the Franco-German philosopher Emile Meyerson. Meyerson's major work, *Identity and Reality*, taught Piaget that there was a way to fuse logic and time. Meyerson wrote that identity was the logical foundation of thought. Piaget realized that there had to be something more than the principle of identity to account for learning. Piaget found his answer in the idea of equilibrium or a reciprocal balancing in the organizational interactions among the parts of a structure (Balestra, 1980).

Another philosopher who influenced Piaget directly was Auguste Sabatier. Sabatier rejected established, denominational Christianity. Sabatier advocated a "scientific" theology that would use logic and scientific investigation to discover theological truths. Thus, Sabatier advocated a notion of "evolution of dogma" (Balestra, p. 414). "Sabatier studied all phenomena in their natural succession and taught Piaget to observe each fact as it appears because the order of the appearance determined its truth and value" (Vidal, 1994, p. 127).

However, it was the influence of Arnold Raymond that led Piaget to abandon Bergsonism (Piaget, 1966a), although not the free-thinking theology of Sabatier. Reymond was a professor of philosophy at Neuchatel's gymnasium and university. He carried out studies on Greek science while also teaching philosophy, the philosophy of science, psychology, mathematics, and logic. Reymond was a colleague of Piaget's father and was also Piaget's mathematics professor. His lectures "left Piaget with a lasting respect for the value of a historic-critical approach and the need for an interdisciplinary work" (Balestra, 1980, p. 420). Reymond's holistic approach to understanding mathematics was instrumental in the development of genetic epistemology because Reymond showed Piaget that logic could provide the key to discovering the evolution of human thinking (Balestra, 1980).

Piaget always considered Reymond one of his masters, and it was Reymond's persuasion that persuaded Piaget to reject Freud and Jung (Piaget, 1952). Reymond demonstrated to Piaget that the problem of a biological species is approachable as a logical problem. What Reymond failed to do, however, was to provide the concrete experimental grounding that would prove his ideas correct—that Piaget's experiences in Paris would provide.

Vygotsky

Vygotsky received his interest in Hegel and Kant from his father. Vygotsky built his cultural–historical theory on Hegel's idea of the dialectic and Kant's idea of the will and perception. Influenced by Marxism during the Russian Revolution, "Vygotsky put learning into a historic and cultural context" (Daniels, 1993, p. 18) because "that is how Karl Marx presented communism" (Razmyslov, 1934, pp. 78–86). This idea of dialectical materialism became integral to Vygotsky's theory on language as a tool of social and learning activity because Vygotsky believed that Leninism "called for the bolshevization of the disciplines" (Daniels, 1993, p. 205). In addition, in an effort to bring psychology into line with Marx's dialectal materialism, Vygotsky saw consciousness as a human labor activity. He theorized that learning was social in origin and evolutionary in scope in order to endorse Marx and Engels's social determination theory as written in their *Sixth Thesis on Feuerbach* (Wertsch, 1985). Vygotsky would also see language as a tool for mental activity in order to make language an analogue of Marx's "kapital" (Wertsch, 1985, p. 49).

During Lenin's rule, communism promised freedom. Indeed, the doors that were closed to Vygotsky during czarists' times now were opened. For example, he could now teach in a public school and Kornilov invited Vygotsky to work with him in Moscow. This new freedom made Vygotsky "embrace Marxism" (Yaroshevsky, 1996, Introduction). While Gita Vygodskaya claimed in 1988 that her father was "always a soviet" (Vygodskaya, 1994/1996, p. 1), some researchers believe that it wasn't until Vygotsky returned to Gomel after his brother's death in Kiev that Vygotsky had time enough to reflect and decide to embrace communism. Vygotsky's earlier experience with Hegel made this not difficult to do. Once Vygotsky decided to accept communism, he had to defend it. Vygotsky put learning into a historic and cultural context because that is how Marx presented communism (Razmyslov, 1934).

Conclusion

Both men made the decision early in their lives to reject their organized religion in favor of philosophy. Piaget, while a teenager, decided to reform philosophy of its irrational nature through use of science's logic. Vygotsky, while a young man, decided to embrace communism. Both men were well read in philosophy and were heavily influenced by it.

RELIGION

Piaget and Vygotsky were raised in moderately religious families that encouraged free thinking. However, by the time they started their professional careers, both men would reject the established, formal faith of their childhoods. Nevertheless, the values that those faiths imparted in early childhood would stay with these men their entire lives and be instrumental in the creation of their respective learning theories.

Piaget's Protestantism had an "intense individualism" (Van Biema, 1908, p. 80), so it is not unusual for Piaget to endorse individualism in his pedagogy. Judaism values society. It is the social milieu that educates and nurtures the individual. The individual functions within a social milieu; thus, Vygotsky would discover the need for a "social other" and a social context for learning. Nevertheless, raised in faiths that valued good education, it is not surprising that both Piaget and Vygotsky would strive to improve education though the creation of their pedagogies.

Piaget

Piaget's French-Protestant Calvinism influenced him to try to help others. He believed in Calvin's work ethic and modeled the virtue of hard work his entire life. As a Christian socialist, Piaget wanted to find scientific reasons for morality, and that is why he embarked on the effort to create genetic epistemology (Piaget, 1952).

In 1983, Paul Sants wrote "Jean Piaget's Attitudes to Education," which appeared in *Jean Piaget: An Interdisciplinary Critique*. According to Sants, Piaget's French-Protestant Christianity and the influence of Christian teachers and mentors prompted his work and led to the conception of his ideas. It was the combined Christian influence of Piaget's family, clubs, friends, mentors, and church—especially the studies for confirmation— that led Piaget into epistemology. In Piaget's hometown, youth often had a crisis of faith. But the Christian people that surrounded Piaget enlarged this crisis. Because of two nervous breakdowns (in 1915 and during the winter of 1917–1918), Piaget would discover accommodation and equilibration. Noting how the mollusks and snails adapted to environmental crises in the Neuchatel Museum of Natural History's laboratory (Isaaca, 1974), Piaget used the example of perception of a problem, internalizing the problem, and acting out a solution to the problem to overcome both mental breakdowns. The first crisis resulted in his *The Mission and the Idea*, in which he rejected a personal Christian God in favor of a wedding of philosophy with science. The second crisis resulted in *Reschere* in which he decided to eliminate the irrational from philosophy, and the heart of philosophy is epistemology (Piaget, 1976). The problem was, Piaget reasoned, that philosophy was not rational. He would use his knowledge of science, which he deemed rational, to purge philosophy, and theology, of its irrational nature.

Fernando Vidal (1989) held it was Piaget's Christian beliefs that motivated him to create an epistemology that was "a moral enterprise aimed at making possible human individual and social salvation" (p. 190). Piaget was an offspring of Swiss Protestantism, which was highly liberal at the time. As such, Piaget "shared with many of his peers the ideal of modeling himself upon the heroic image of Jesus Christ" (Vidal, 1989, p. 191). The destruction of World War I caused followers of this liberal Protestantism to attempt an establishment of a new order that saw faith as governed by the same psychological laws that governed other human experiences. Vidal cited Piaget's prose, *The Mission of the Idea*, as proof that this interpretation was correct. This poem castigated intellectualism as a betrayal of the mission of theology and called upon the idealism of youth to meet the challenges of wartime circumstances. In that 1915 work, Piaget saw himself as the young man who was to work for the realization of the Idea [a Christian epistemology] on earth. "Honor to him who meditates, alone, in his silent room, and then thrusts into full light the young idea that will dash through the world, as the storm agitates the sea" (Piaget, 1915, p. 11).

Thus, Piaget replaced theology with philosophy; specifically, a philosophy purified by science. However, his faith never fully left him. While Piaget rejected organized theology, the basis or heart of that theology (mainly, its roots or ethics) would form the basis of genetic epistemology.

Vygotsky

Young Lev Vygotsky received a traditional Jewish education, reading the Torah in Hebrew, delivering a speech at his bar mitzvah, and so on. "The frequent references in his work to the Bible can be understood in this context" (van der Veer & Valsiner, 1991, p. 4).

Vygotsky became interested in Jewish culture at an early age and started to identify to some extent with the history of the Jewish people (Vygotsky, 1916). External circumstances encouraged this interest. For example, Vygotsky witnessed the ignominious return of the Jewish members of the Russian army to Gomel. This return took place after an incorrect rumor had been spread that Jewish soldiers were not trustworthy in wartime (Levitin, 1982, p. 27). Lenin demanded that true soviets reject organized religion.

Vygotsky spent 7 years in Gomel as a schoolteacher pondering what to do about his faith. With Lenin opening up avenues of opportunity to those who agreed to be soviets, Vygotsky would reject his formal Jewish religion, but the precepts that it taught him would remain within him (Vygodskaya, 1984). Judaism is a very ethical, socially concerned theology. These roots of his faith would remain with Vygotsky his entire life. This, plus his interest in his Jewish heritage, would blend with other experiences in Vygotsky's life to create his idea of the sociocultural–historical context of learning.

Conclusion

Both Vygotsky and Piaget may have rejected the man-made aspects of their respective theologies, but they never rejected the heart of their faiths. However, recognizing that their nations could improve the lives of their people, both men chose education as the method by which this could occur. This drive to improve their nation's education was encouraged by what happened within that field in their own lives.

ART/EDUCATION

Except for the written word, art did not influence either Piaget or Vygotsky. Developing good writing and thinking skills is part of a good education. Both men received two types of education: formal and informal. The formal and informal education that Piaget and Vygotsky received was excellent, but it was the informal education that gave both of them the valuable skill of being able to write well. Without this skill, they could not have conveyed their ideas adequately enough for those ideas to be accepted.

Like Piaget, Vygotsky started writing at an early age. Both men wrote their first works at 10 years of age. Vygotsky first wrote an analysis of Tolstoy's *Anna Karenina*. Unfortunately, this first essay was destroyed during World War II when the Germans attacked Gomel in 1943, but the knowledge that it gave would help Vygotsky write his dissertation. The first writing of Vygotsky that survived is his critique of Shakespeare's *Hamlet*. This was started when he was 10 years old but was not finished until he was 19 (Blanck, 1990) and would become the subject for his doctoral dissertation *The History of Art*.

Piaget would write about an albino sparrow. It was published despite his young age and Piaget recalled that "I was launched!" (Piaget, 1952). Outside of teaching him how to write well, the arts did not influence Piaget, but they did have a profound influence on Vygotsky.

Vygotsky received his love of literature from his mother. Vygotsky's childhood "play" built upon that love. Vygotsky would put on dramas and hold literary discussions and debates with his sister Zinaida, brother Dodik, and "troika friends" David and Dobkin. There were many family readings of great literature around the dining room samovar during the long winter evenings. In addition, Vygotsky, his siblings, and his friends took advantage of the public library that Vygotsky's parents created in town. So, Vygotsky was able to immerse himself in the well-written word early in his life and this would foster his idea that language was the tool of learning.

Formal education was to have a remarkable impact on both Piaget's and Vygotsky's ideas. This is especially true when considering Piaget's and Vygotsky's higher education. I believe that without their university studies, both men would have remained as either an excellent natural scientist (Piaget) or a great teacher in literary analysis (Vygotsky). This is because, at their universities, psychology was part of the discipline in which both men were getting their degrees. Without psychology being considered part of philosophy at the University of Zurich and without psychology being considered part of history and philology at the two universities in Moscow, Piaget and Vygotsky would never have been able to create their respective pedagogues.

Fernando Vidal, in his 1994 book, *Piaget Before Piaget*, points out that Piaget "was enrolled at the University of Zurich, in the department called Philosophy I, during the 1918–19 winter term (October to March). The professors he [Piaget] mentions in connection with experimental psychology, Arthur Wreschner...and Gotthold-Friedrich Lipps...also taught courses in philosophy, pedagogy, and mental development" (Vidal, 1994, p. 224).

Mikhail Yaroshevski explained in his 1994 work, *Vygotsky and His Position on Psychological Sciences,* that psychology in those days meant the study of individual consciousness, and because of this, the analysis of literature was part of psychology. The Institute of Psychology opened as part of Moscow (earlier Imperial) University's Department of History and Philology the same year that Vygotsky became a student there. The psychologists shared the same campus building with the historians and philologists. Therefore, because of his interest in the humanities and because literary analysis was considered part of psychology, becoming a psychologist was not that big of a move for Vygotsky to make.

In addition, Vygotsky also studied simultaneously at Shanaivsky University. His primary interest was literary criticism. At that university, psychology was "taken to mean the study of individual consciousness" (Yaroshevski, 1994, p. 35). This consciousness also expanded to art, history, and literature.

Vygotsky would expand the study of individual consciousness while at Shana-ivsky University to the study of the individual's dependence on the historical development of world culture (Yaroshevsky, 1996). Thus, it was a natural or logical step for Vygotsky to move from literary criticism to the study of how learning takes place in a sociohistorical context.

Two teachers impacted Vygotsky and his ideas in a very important manner. The first teacher was Solomon Ashpiz because his Socratic method of teaching opened the door for Vygotsky to attend the universities in Moscow. Ashpiz's teaching endorsed four ideas that Vygotsky had started to form in his childhood that would become major factors within sociohistorical theory, namely, language as a tool of learning, the "social other" as a factor for learning, the ZPD, and the sociohistorical context of learning. The other teacher was Gustav Shpet. He was a professor at Shanaivsky University who finalized for Vygotsky the psychological aspects of language. Now, Vygotsky had the words to go with his ideas to form the concept of language as a tool of learning. Without these two teachers, Vygotsky might never have conceived of cultural–historical theory.

Piaget

Piaget attended the local Latin School. He then went on to the University of Neuchatel where he received his baccalaureate in natural sciences and became ABD (all but dissertation) in philosophy. Piaget's classroom teachers were ineffective (Piaget, 1952). Despite this, there were those in the community who took over Piaget's informal education. This was a good thing because Piaget felt that his early formal education was not that helpful to him, but it was his informal education that taught him how to think and organize. Thus, Piaget benefited much more from his informal education than Vygotsky. Piaget's first literary critic was his father, who criticized two of Piaget's early works. Piaget's informal education also included all the work that he did for Paul Godet, who was director of Neuchatel's Museum of Natural History and who hired the young man to help him in his mollusk department (paying him in specimens). This work, besides classifying specimens (i.e., extra mollusks and snails for Piaget's own personal collection) for Godet, included solitary learning. Piaget did his first independent research, field investigations, and writing while under the tutelage of Godet.

When he became a teenager, the Jura Club and Friends of Nature also encouraged and applauded Piaget's independent biological research. In his autobiographies, Piaget wrote that the classroom was a "frustrating place" (Sants, 1983, p. 89). There was no independent study. Self regulation, it can be seen, had appealed to Piaget "at a very early age" (Piaget, 1952, p. 352). However, because of his unhappiness with his formal education at the Latin School, Piaget would write "against trying to transform the child's mind from the outside by authoritarian means" (Sants, 1983, p. 90). In his 1932 work, entitled *Moral Judgment of the Child*, Piaget would write, "It is idle. . .to try and transform the child's mind from outside, when his own taste for active research and his desire for cooperation suffice to ensure normal intellectual development" (p. 392).

Piaget's argument against traditional classrooms may have its origin in his unhappy home life, because Piaget would also write against parental instruction. "Parental 'mistakes' can only too easily disturb [sic]. Much better for the child's social interaction to be with 'collaborators'" (Piaget, 1932, p. 393). Thus, because of his unhappy experience with most formalized teaching (be it at home or in the traditional classroom), Piaget would form the concept of an inactive teacher who would allow the child to engage in independent study. Piaget called this idea self-regulation.

Piaget's teacher was to correctly create a "classroom environment that was set at the child's stage of development" (Sants, 1983, p. 88). Piaget successfully tested this idea when he was a diagnostician in Paris after graduating from the University of Neuchatel and also when he did a semester's work at the University of Zurich.

Vygotsky

Vygotsky also benefited as much from a good informal education as he did his formal one. It was his early formal education that taught him how to think and analyze. By the time he was 15 years old, Vygotsky earned the title "the little professor" (Blanck, 1990, p. 34) because he had generated intellectual discussions among his friends. Because of the ZPDs set up by his parents and the later ZPDs set up by both his "troika" and siblings, Vygotsky's interests in theater, history, and philosophy were integrated early (Blanck, 1990). During the same time period, Fanya and Semyon Dobkin (neighborhood friends) and Zinaida, Vygotsky's sister, invited him to preside over a Jewish history circle. "This activity lasted for two years and eventually led to the study of the philosophy of history" (Blanck, 1990, p. 34). This study, when coupled with the study of Hegel that his father had already introduced him to, must have stimulated his adherence to Marx—a connection not at all arbitrary (Cohen, 1976).

As stated earlier, Vygotsky was able to win the Gold Medal and entrance into the university in Moscow because of the education given to him by his childhood tutor, Solomon Asphiz, who taught by the Socratic method. This method (coupled with the informal learning activities of his youth) was to later result in both the concept of the ZPD (Wertsch, 1985) and contributed to Vygotsky's idea that language is the tool of learning (Rissom, 1985;

Wertsch, 1985). Vygotsky, early in his youth, was able to accept the concepts of the "social other" and scaffolding (after invented by Jerome Bruner) because of Asphiz's teaching skill (Dobkin, 1982). "It was Ashpiz's pedagogical technique which influenced Vygotsky to recognize the use of language by the "social other" can promote well-developed, inquisitive minds" (Wertsch, 1985, p. 4).

"No more than 3 percent of student bodies [either at the Imperial University of Moscow or Saint Petersburg University] could be Jewish" (Wertsch, 1985, p. 5). Once enrolled, Vygotsky obtained a law degree from the Imperial University of Moscow (Newman & Holzman, 1993) and a degree in literary analysis from Shanaivsky University. Next door to the Imperial University of Moscow was the Psychological Institute in which Ivan Schenov researched reflexive behavior. Vygotsky attended Schenov's lectures. Schenov's ideas would lead Vygotsky, when he began his own research in the Gomel psychological laboratory that he built, into terming "cognition as...the reflex of reflexes" (Yaroshevski, 1996, p. 38). This led Vygotsky into delivering his 1924 paper at the Second Psychoneurological Congress. This address, as earlier explained, resulted in an invitation to work at the Psychological Institute in Moscow—and a place in history.

Vygotsky also enrolled in a new Moscow university called Shanaivsky University. This was an unofficial school that sprang up after the Czar's Minister of Education expelled most of the students "in a crackdown on an anti czarist [sic] movement" (Wertsch, 1985, p. 6). In protest, more than a hundred professors walked out after the students' expulsion and created a free-thinking university (Dobkin, 1982). Since literary analysis, philology, and history always interested Vygotsky, he enrolled in Shanaivksy University to study those subjects. "Vygotsky gained much more from the atmosphere of that university [Shanaivsky] and from mixing with the students and teachers there than from his studies at the law department" (Dobkin, 1982, p. 30). The professors, especially Dr. Gustav Shpet, encouraged Vygotsky to write about the role of the "social other." That role would contain the goal of enabling students to internalize information given by the "social other" and that ability would enable the student to create a new, and improved, construct (Wertsch, 1985).

At Shanaivsky University, Vygotsky also picked up the idea that, thanks to the "social other," society and cognition created an active, ever-upward evolutionary spiral of knowledge. Also while attending that university, Vygotsky and his sister Zinaida attended lessons by Shpet, who was a noted student of Humboldt. Those lessons sensitized Vygotsky to the psychological aspects of language (van der Veer & Valsiner, 1991). Vygotsky remembered that, as a teenager, he had read Potebnya's book entitled *Thought and Language*. This book was Vygotsky's first acquaintance with psychology. Potebnya's ideas about language as the microcosm of thought and as an instrument of constructing man's inner world "guided Vygotsky's future studies" (Yaroshevski, 1996, p. 36). Vygotsky wedded Potebny's ideas with the teachings of Shpet to give birth to the idea that communication (through reading, hearing, or observing body language) was the tool of instruction.

Conclusion

In conclusion, it was the education of Piaget and Vygotsky that gave them the means by which they could relieve their inner psychological tensions through the development of the new ideas that compose their respective theories. The observation of their respective intellectual expansions allows one to trace the origin of their ideas.

THE ORIGIN OF PIAGET'S IDEAS

Equilibration

"Equilibration is similar to Vygotsky's idea of internalization" (Steffe, 1995, p. 510; Hamilton, 1997). Piaget developed this idea while in the Swiss mountains recuperating from two mental breakdowns. This idea was endorsed by the philosophers introduced to him by his father, godfather, and own personal readings. He was able to formalize this idea in his mind when he both worked and studied in Paris. The final confirmation came when he worked at the Rousseau Institute and was able to test his idea in a controlled classroom environment.

Chronological Stages of Development

While still in his early childhood at Neuchatel, Piaget developed the idea of organisms' learning progressing chronologically by observing the reaction of mollusks and snails at the Neuchatel Museum of Natural History. These observations were expanded with his adolescent clubs, especially the Friends of Nature.

The works of Darwin, Bergson, Sabatier, and other researchers mentioned in the economic and philosophical discussions of this intellectual curve confirmed these earlier observations. It was while he was in Paris, however, that Piaget was able to bridge the zoological with the human so that when he was at the Jean-Jacques Rousseau Institute, Piaget could set definite age levels to his human stages of cognitive development.

The seed for the idea of cognitive readiness was planted in the Neucha-tel laboratory, but came into its own when Piaget was diagnosing young-sters in Paris to finish a cognitive readiness test that Dr. Burt had started under the directorship of Drs. Simon and Binet. The environment condu-cive to Piaget's cognitive readiness is similar to Vygotsky's ZPD (Hamilton, 1988). However, the development of this idea came from Piaget's contact with Reymond, Jung, and Arnold. Piaget proved this idea correct through his work for Claparede.

Language

Both Vygotsky and Piaget had a role for language. Piaget believed that social interaction was not as important as inner speech (Davydoiv & Radz-ikhovsky, 1985). He also believed that the use of language during instruction can show a lack of operative thinking (Piaget, 1962). However, he received the idea that the teacher could use language as a way to diagnose the correct classroom learning environment from his experiences; first, working in Paris and, second, in Geneva working for the Jean-Jacques Rousseau Institute.

Teacher as Diagnostician

Piaget, unlike Vygotsky, was never a classroom teacher. Furthermore, Piaget's experience at the Latin School was less than happy. However, with his work both in Paris and later, at the Jean-Jacques Rousseau Institute, Piaget confirmed the idea set in his childhood at the Latin School that the teacher should only function as a diagnostician—not an active instructor. Furthermore, unlike the impoverished USSR, Piaget's Switzerland was prosperous enough to enable a teacher to provide an intellectually stimu-lating classroom environment. Vygotsky had to rely on a cheaper method of instruction; namely, paying a teacher to use language to scaffold a child up to the height of that child's ZPD.

Error

Piaget saw error as part of the learning process (Forman, 1980). In sci-entific experiments, error is an acceptable outcome. Often, it is as impor-tant to prove something incorrect as to prove it correct in a research study. It is not considered a failure if the positive hypothesis is proven incorrect through objective, scientific investigation. Therefore, Piaget, who used sci-ence to form a rational epistemology, would evolve the idea that error is allowable. Piaget reasoned that failure in life or education is not to be avoided. One can perhaps learn more from one's mistakes than one's accomplishments. He learned this when his father rejected Piaget's idea of the *Autovap* at age 8 and his *Our Birds* a year later. The result was that Piaget tried harder and, when only 10, his *Un Moineu Albinœ* was published as an adult work. Piaget's idea was confirmed, however, not only in his life experiences, but also with his work both in Paris and at the Jean-Jacques Rousseau Institute. By the time Piaget became a professor of psychology, sociology, and the philosophy of science at the University of Neuchatel in 1925, this idea was in place.

On a personal note, Piaget's own hospitalizations demonstrated to him that conflict was essential for growth. Without his first nervous breakdown in 1915, he would not have accepted the attempt to purify philosophy, through the use of science, of its irrational factors. Without his second nervous breakdown starting in 1917, perhaps he would not have discovered the ideas of equilibration and accommodation. Thus, error or conflict to Piaget was part of life's processes and could result in better ideas.

Independence of the Learner

Piaget concentrated on the child doing independent inquiry in the classroom to reach the top of that child's stage of chronological development. Although Piaget had earlier allowed the teacher to give limited instruction, once Stalin began his reign of terror in the USSR, Piaget reversed himself and limited the teacher to just being a diagnostician (Piaget 1966a, 1976). Piaget's own development in childhood was that of the solitary inquirer. He was successful, and his experience in both Paris and at the Jean-Jacques Rousseau Institute demonstrated that other children could also be successful using this method. The Swiss are known to value their freedom. Vygotsky's concept of the "social other" could allow for Stalinist dictatorships over young minds and Piaget was against that. The birth of this idea, therefore, took place in Piaget's childhood but developed with his postgraduate work in Paris and Geneva.

Optimal Mismatch

Piaget's optimal mismatch corresponds to Vygotsky's idea of "scaffolding" as explained by Jerome Bruner (Bruner, 1967; Kuhn, 1979). The optimal mismatch takes place when the challenge is placed at the top of the child's stage of chronological development. The tension that occurs from this demanding task results in the child rising higher intellectually, by solving the difficult problem. Piaget first developed this idea while working in the Neuchatel Museum of Natural History. However, this idea bloomed to fruition first in Paris with his investigations for Burt's test and, second, with his work at the Jean-Jacques Rousseau Institute. Piaget faced his own problems and solved them by using the optimal mismatch. The inner "angst" caused by his childhood family relationships did result in creativity.

Play

Unstructured play was considered a waste of time and dangerous by Piaget (G. DeVoogd, personal communication, March 1998). Piaget himself wrote that early in his life he rejected play for work to imitate his father, who was suffering from a psychotic spouse, as well as to provide a peaceful refuge for himself (Piaget, 1952). Brian Sutton-Smith, in his 1979 book entitled *Play and Learning*, wrote that it was Piaget's Calvinism with its work ethic that made Piaget write that students should forego play as soon as possible for structured classroom learning. This made Piaget so incensed that he wrote a paper entitled *Response to Brian Sutton-Smith* in 1966, angrily refuting such an idea. In that article and in his book, *Comments,* Piaget wrote that play can open the mind to unstructured, fictional thinking. Irrational thinking can open the door to mental illness.

THE ORIGIN OF VYGOTSKY'S IDEAS

Zone of Proximal Development (ZPD)

Vygotsky's parents, siblings, friends, tutors, and mentors established with him zones of proximal development. This is "similar to Piaget's chronological stages of development" (Wertsch & Tulviste, 1992, p. 553), except that Vygotsky placed no actual age constraints. Vygotsky admitted experiencing ZPDs throughout his life but decided to publish the idea after reading two of Piaget's books that were originally published in French in 1923 and 1924. The result was Vygotsky's 1926 work, *Pedagogicheskaj & Psikhlogija*. In this work, Vygotsky refused to set chronological age limits to his stages of development and also acknowledged that some societies might never reach the highest stage (Wertsch, 1985) due to their primitiveness.

Vygotsky's ZPD developed along with his idea on internalization. It was born by his parents in the nurturing, learning environment that they created for their children (and later expanded to their children's friends) in Gomel. Gomel itself was a larger ZPD with many cultural and learning activities for its citizens. The entire Vygotsky family, including Lev, contributed to this atmosphere. Besides this, Vygotsky on his own set up his first troika with his cousin, brother, and neighbor. Vygotsky's personal education was nothing short of a ZPD experience: first, under Aspiz; second, at the Gomel private Jewish gymnasium; and third, in Moscow—first as a student and, second, with Leontiev and Luria. Vygotsky also set up ZPDs in Gomel when he taught either high school students or adults. All of these ZPDs were successful and, so, when Vygotsky decided to publish on this idea, everything was in place but the name. Despite this experience in his personal life, Vygotsky modestly stated that his concept of the ZPD was not original but rather developed from American investigators, including "the work of the American, Dorothea McCarthy" (Kozyrev & Turko, 1935, pp. 44–57).

Internalization

Vygotsky's idea of internalization was born during his family's ZPDs around the family samovar in the dining room during the long Russian winters It developed during the literary sessions that transpired as childhood play with his friends and siblings. His first tutor, Solomon Aspiz, successfully used this method to train Vygotsky so that when he entered his private Jewish gymnasium for only 2 years of education, he was able to obtain the gold medal given for the best scholar. In addition, the philosophies of Hegel, introduced by Vygotsky's father to him, and the Gestalt psychologists, which he studied after graduating from his two universities, also endorsed this idea. Internalization was further formalized as a teacher in Gomel (both in the classroom and in his psychological laboratory that he set up there). However, it was endorsed after Vygotsky read Piaget's 1923 book, *Le Judgement et le Raisonment Chez Infant*. Finally, Vygotsky also read Bergson and Darwin. Those two authors further endorsed Vygotsky's idea of internalization.

Stages of Development

Vygotsky had the idea that a child's intellect goes through stages of development from looking at his own education. After reading Piaget, Vygotsky decided to publish his own idea about stages of development. However, his postgraduate work at the Gomel high school and teachers' college convinced Vygotsky that, unlike Piaget, he should not set chronological ages as boundaries for those stages. Vygotsky also postulated that some people do not reach the highest stage, not because they are not capable of reaching it, but because they did not have the opportunity to do so

(Wertsch & Tulviste, 1992). The idea of stages of development was born through introspection into his own childhood. Literary analysis also shows how an author internalizes an idea in a great work to reach a literary climax, and Vygotsky did a lot of literary analysis. Thus, it was a combination of childhood experiences, literary analysis, and Piaget's idea that prompted Vygotsky to create his stages of development.

Originally, Vygotsky postulated that there were only three stages of development, because this is what he observed in his Gomel teachers' academy. These were precausality, secondary differentiation, and differentiation. However, after reading Piaget, and writing the introduction to the Russian translation of Piaget's 1923 book, *Language and Thought of the Child*, Vygotsky increased his stages to mirror Piaget's four. To do this, Vygotsky divided his first stage into two. These became primary differentiation and real instrumental. Learning from Piaget's diagnosis approach to pedagogy, Vygotsky then advocated what he called "dynamic assessment," during which the learner is not also being taught, he is also being assessed. This approach taught Vygotsky during his self-imposed exile from Moscow after Kornilov's execution that, due to the primitiveness of some cultures, the last stage of development was not always obtained.

The "Social Other"

Piaget and Vygotsky differ most on the role of the teacher (Kuhn, 1979). Piaget would reject Vygotsky's idea of the "social other" because throughout Piaget's childhood and adolescence, anyone assigned by Piaget's society to nurture and educate him failed to do so. Vygotsky, on the other hand, experienced his "social others" not only educating him but also saving his life during pogroms, and preparing him successfully for an almost impossible task, a Jew receiving admission to the Imperial University of Moscow. In short, until his Leont'ev-Luria troika betrayed him during one of Stalin's purges, Vygotsky had never experienced an unsuccessful "social other." By that time, however, Vygotsky had already done research and published on this idea. He died soon after the betrayal and, therefore, never refuted it.

The idea of the "social other" resulted from personal experiences that took place by all people assigned by his society to nurture and educate him. This would include Vygotsky's parents, siblings, friends, hometown, education, and the Jewish culture.

Role of Communication

Both Piaget and Vygotsky accepted a role for language in education (Davydov & Radzkowvsky, 1985; Luria, 1982; Yaroshevsky, 1996). Piaget, however, would end up rejecting Vygotsky's stronger role because it showed a lack, in Piaget's opinion, of operative thinking (Piaget, 1962). "Piaget's reluctance to view language as one of the good things of development goes back to his early suspicion that it is the language of adult constraint which confines the child within himself" (Modgil, Modgil, & Brown, 1983, p. 91) and makes it possible for a dictator to control a child's mind. However, Vygotsky's egocentric speech is very content oriented, and he wrote that the content of language is critical to leading a child to newer and better constructs (Davydov & Radzkowvsky, 1985).

Vygotsky's idea of the importance of communication in learning was born in his family's ZPDs. His mother encouraged him to read, and his father encouraged him to analyze philosophy. The Jewish culture also values writing and reading. Later, Vygotsky's siblings, extended family, and friends would use language in their ZPDs to promote culture and learning among its members. Vygotsky spoke and read in six languages. Aspiz, his first tutor, used the art of questioning to lead a student to the correct answer and this is called the Socratic method. This use of language created a smart pupil capable of winning the gold medal after only 2 years at a 4-year gymnasium. Shpet confirmed what Aspiz did when Vygotsky was a university student because Shpet used that same method. Grateful that the Russian Revolution opened the doors to freedom for Russia's Jews, Vygotsky searched for a way to prove Marx's dialectical materialism correct. After wedding Hegel with his own personal experiences, Vygotsky formalized in Gomel after his return from Kiev that communication was the tool of learning.

Error

Vygotsky wrote that error or failure occurs when the social other is not doing a correct, nurturing job; that is, incorrectly passing on the solutions that the student's society has found over time. In Vygotsky's country, making mistakes could get you killed. The persecutions, pogroms, wars, and purges did not leave much room for error. So, while Piaget could accept the concept of error because Switzerland was a peaceful, democratic country and because the scientific research process (that Piaget engaged often in) accepted it, Vygotsky could not. Furthermore, Piaget's two hospitalizations proved to him that error, or conflict, was essential for intellectual growth, but Vygotsky's own experience with two pogroms while still a child and his own father's trial for defending his family, convinced him at an early age that error was to be avoided (Forman, 1980, p. 284). Finally, Marx did not provide for error, and if Vygotsky was going to prove Marxism correct, he also could not provide for error.

Sociohistorical Context of Learning

The second idea that Piaget and Vygotsky differ very strongly on is the context of learning. Piaget, especially after Stalin started his reign of terror, was adamant about the teacher being just a diagnostician and the student being independent of the teacher's personal instruction (Piaget, 1966a, 1976; Steffe & Gale, 1995). Piaget's father was a historian; so, Piaget was exposed to this field of study not only in school, where it was taught with a lot of boring memorization of dates and names, but also at home. Nevertheless, Piaget's own father discouraged him from studying history because "it was too introspective" (Vidal, 1994). Meanwhile, Vygotsky, steeped in history from both his education and Jewish background, would insist that learning is done in a sociohistorical context (Bandura, 1986; Kuhn, 1979).

Vygotsky's idea about the sociohistorical context of learning was born in his Jewish historical studies, his personal reading of other histories, and his education in history starting with his private tutors and ending with his education at Shanaivsky University with his reading of works on evolution, history of philosophy, and communism. Thus, Kant, Hegel, Darwin, Spencer, Spinoza, Marx, and Engels formalized an idea that Vygotsky had developed as an adolescent.

Scaffolding

Scaffolding is a term that was not used by Vygotsky, even though Vygotsky conceptualized the idea. It was first used by Jerome Bruner (1967) to describe a student being brought from the bottom of his stage of development to the top by a caring "social other" through the use of communication. Bruner was the first author to see the similarities between Piaget and Vygotsky. Scaffolding is very "similar to Piaget's idea of the optimal mismatch" (Kuhn, 1979, p. 356). In Piaget's idea, a classroom environment is set at the highest challenging point for a student's chronological stage of development so that, with effort, a child can move, if the child successfully internalizes the problem, through equilibration to the top of that child's stage of development (Hamilton, 1997).

For Vygotsky, this sociohistorical context of learning continues generation after generation to create a society whose learning is spiraling ever upward as one generation builds upon the learning of the other; thus, societies are scaffolding upward as well. Vygotsky developed this idea from a lifetime of experiences: his parents, his siblings, his cousins, his friends, his hometown, and his jobs. With his interest in the philosophers mentioned in this chapter, it was not difficult for Vygotsky to take those personal experiences and wed them with Marx's philosophy of history. Vygotsky did this to prove Marx correct and, also, it neatly dovetailed with Vygotsky's idea on the role of communication in learning (Bruner, 1967).

Play

The third idea in which Piaget and Vygotsky differ the most is their idea of play (DeVoogd, 1997). Piaget saw play as only acceptable as an early life experience (babyhood), and believed that it was a waste of time after that stage of development. It was unstructured thinking, and that could lead to madness (Piaget, 1962, 1966a). Vygotsky, on the other hand, because of his personal experiences while growing up in Gomel with his family, friends, and hometown's ZPDs, believed that play was a great learning experience. Indeed, Vygotsky's childhood play was a valuable learning experience (Vygotsky, 1967).

CONCLUSIONS

There are three schools of thought on both Piaget and Vygotsky and all three evolve around why the pedagogists invented their pedagogies. The three schools are thesis, antithesis, and synthesis. Writers of the three schools include both theorists and historians. There have been a few biographies written on either Piaget or Vygotsky, but no one has written a biographical comparison of both men. Also, no one has looked at the impact of their personal lives on the formation of all their main ideas.

Piaget

The thesis school on Piaget includes biographers and theorists who claim that Piaget invented genetic epistemology because of an interest in biology that developed into a desire to create an evolution of learning much like Darwin created his biological evolution of the species. This school was started by both Henri Pieron and Nathan Isaaca and includes

James Wertsch, Read Tuddenham, Margaret Boden, Richard Evans, Maurice Van der Goot, and Merete Amann-Gainotti.

The revisionist school of historical thought on Jean Piaget says that it was the desire to cleanse philosophy of the irrational that led to the creation of genetic epistemology. Writers of this school include early Piaget, Brian Sutton-Smith, Ellizabeth Hall, Dominic Balestra, Rita Vuyk, Lynn Liben, Paul Sants, Michael Chapman, Leslie Smith, and Fernando Vidal.

The synthesis school of thought on Piaget said that it was both to advance science and improve philosophy that caused Piaget to create his pedagogy. Writers of this school include later Piaget, Jean-Claude Bringuier, Howard Gruber, J. Jacques Vonche, Leslie Smith, Thomas Kesselring, Alberto Munari, Jean-Marc Barrelet, Anne-Nelly Perret-Clermont, Jacques Montangero, Danielle Maurice-Naville, Jean-Jacques Ducret, and Maurice Tribolet.

Vygotsky

The thesis school of historical thought on Vygotsky believes that he created cultural–historical theory to prove Marxism correct. Authors of this school include James Wertsch, Ingrid Rissom, Harry Daniels, Fred Newman, Lois Holzman, Semen Dobkin, Gita Vygotskaya, A.R. Luria, and A.V. Zaporozhetz.

The antithesis school believes that Vygotsky created his pedagogy to reform psychology. Writers of this school include Michael Cole, Jerome Bruner, Carl Ratner, Fred Newman, Lois Holzman, and Mikail Yaroshevsky.

The synthesis school of historical thought states that it was both to endorse Marxism and reform psychology that Vygotsky created cultural–historical theory. Writers in this school include Guillermo Blanck, Rene Van der Veer, Jerome Valsiner, and Alexander Kozulin.

Summation

I believe that both men created their pedagogies to help others going through difficulties. If people could be taught well, they will be able to handle adversity well. I base this idea upon this work. This biographical comparison has shed light on the similarities not only in the personal lives of Jean Piaget and Lev Vygotsky, but also on the similarities of their ideas. Both men and their ideas were products of their time and all the personal life experiences that went with those times. The seeds of their respective ideas were sown in early childhood. Parents, family, and hometown environments are important The ideas that each man had grew during their

formal and informal periods of education. Both men's ideas came to fruition when they did their first postgraduate work. So, by the time they
started their personal careers, those ideas were set and proven in postgraduate employment research opportunities. Thus, both men had an advantage. Both were able to start their professional careers already knowing that
the ideas that they wished to publish on were valid—they just needed the
formal, experimental research to prove so to the world. All of this was
accomplished through extreme adversity that both men overcame. What
they had accomplished had helped them and, now, they wanted to use
their methods of overcoming adversity to help others.

Both men were proven humanitarians. Piaget volunteered his time to
work with the mentally ill and Vygotsky volunteered his time to work in the
field of what he called defectology (those who couldn't see, hear, or were
behaviorally disabled). They wished to prevent or relieve the suffering of
others. The contributions that both made to education can be found not
only in the study of their respective pedagogies, but also in their own personal lives. Indeed, the answers to how teachers can best help those fighting adversity can be found by looking at how Piaget and Vygotsky fought
and triumphed over adversity in their own lives.

CHAPTER 6

THE LESSONS TAUGHT ON HOW TO CONQUER ADVERSITY

INTRODUCTION

If teachers believe that the only thing they have to impart to their students is knowledge of the subject, they need not go any farther than the pedagogies that Piaget and Vygotsky created. If, however, teachers believe that they have responsibility to teach more than the subject, they need to look at the personal lives of both Jean Piaget and Lev Vygotsky. There, they will discover how two young men in the turbulent 20th century were able to overcome extreme difficulties to develop major works that changed worldwide how a child is taught. Their struggles gave them strength and ideas.

Piaget and Vygotsky were leaders in their field. More importantly, their concepts started revolutions in education. There is, until now, no research on how Piaget and Vygotsky managed to overcome their own problems. Also, no one has shown how these men modeled these actions in their own personal lives, until now. Exposing both actions will illuminate methods for teachers dealing with such situations among their own students. "Contemporary authors seem to say little or nothing about what leaders must have done yesterday to become leaders today. Yet, the ground of leadership can lie only in the leader's personal history" (Schaeffer, 1982).

Parallel Paths to Constructivism: Jean Piaget and Lev Vygotsky, pages 95–102
Copyright © 2004 by Information Age Publishing

"Leaders cannot be thought of apart from the historic context in which they arise, the setting in which they function" (Gardner, 1996). Teachers should give young people a sense of the many kinds of leaders and styles of leadership, and encourage them to move toward the models that are right for them. Piaget and Vygotsky provide two such models.

However, before they were leaders, they were humans struggling with difficult situations. "leadership may be chiefly an achievement of follower-servants—that able leaders may emerge only from the ranks of able followers" (Schaeffer, 1982, p. 4). Hegel wrote that the mature leader must have known the travail of the follower, he must here and now incorporate within himself all that the servant is (Schaffer, personal communication, June 13, 1998).

Being a good servant is a necessary condition to being a good leader. Piaget and Vygotsky are examples of such servant-leaders. "Servant-leadership emphasizes increased service to others, a holistic approach to work, promoting a sense of community, and sharing of power in decision making" (Schaffer, personal communication, June 13, 1998). True leadership emerges from those whose primary motivation is a deep desire to help others (Greenleaf, Frick, & Spears, 1996).

Helping both Piaget and Vygotsky were their parents, relatives, and mentors or teachers. The jobs, difficulties, and responsibilities that they faced in their childhood helped them build early in life self-confidence, the willingness to make decisions, and the willingness to stand the consequences (Greenleaf et al., 1996). The most successful people are those who learn early in life these important facts, who have had disruptions (adversity) in their youth, and who have survived (Greenleaf et al., 1996).

Both Piaget and Vygotsky lived in a nurturing environment (i.e., hometown). They conceived their ideas in a culture that was "problem solving"; that is, it was one in which protocol and status were minimized, mistakes were tolerated, colleagues were allies not competitors, and results were rewarded directly and openly (Greenleaf et al., 1996). For Piaget, the problem-solving culture (first in Neuchatel, then in Paris, and finally in Geneva) lasted his whole lifetime. For Vygotsky, the problem-solving culture existed in Gomel and lasted in Russia from the Russian Revolution until Stalin obtained total dictatorship of the USSR in 1929.

Being a leader means that one has a sense of the past but can also think strategically about the future (Slaughter, 1996). Piaget and Vygotsky were able to do both. They could stand at the top of a mountain and see the vast expanse of plain below with no roads on it (Hardy, 1996). They built the roads. Both used their own personal past experiences to create pedagogies that were effective. I believe this is because they were able to distinguish themselves as leaders in at least six aspects: (1) They could think long term and beyond the day's crises; (2) they could reach and influence people beyond their own boundaries; (3) they could grasp their ideas in relationship to larger realities; (4) they put heavy emphasis upon vision, values, motivation, and interaction; (5) they had the political savvy to cope with conflicting requirements from multiple sources; and (6) They could think in terms of renewal, that is, they sought revisions of their ideas from communication with others. These aspects of their leadership required a configuration with which to promote and protect their concepts. The paradigm that they both used was to empower others to work with their ideas and soar (Quinn, Mintzberg, & James, 1988). In other words, each individual can replicate an original idea because each individual is empowered by education to do so. Vygotsky established such a paradigm at the Experimental Psychological Institute in Moscow in 1924. However, Vygotsky continued to expand this configuration to other students and colleagues. When he left Moscow during the purge (and subsequent death) of Kornilov by Stalin, Vygotsky extended this management configuration to other areas of the USSR. This explains how cultural–historical theory survived Stalin's repression to emerge completely intact after the fall of communism in 1990. Piaget established such a paradigm when he went to the University of Neuchatel as a professor of psychology, sociology, and the philosophy of science in 1925. He continued operating out of such a management configuration until his death in 1980. This includes all of his work in Zurich and Geneva, and for the United Nations as director of its International Bureau of Education.

CHARACTERISTICS OF A SERVANT-LEADER

What teachers need to do, if they are going to contribute to the total well-being of their students, is to instill within their charges the following 10 factors that both Piaget and Vygotsky exhibited throughout their lives. Teachers need to adopt all 10 characteristics within themselves so that they can model them for their students. These characteristics are "listening, empathy, healing, awareness, persuasion, conceptualization, foresight, stewardship, commitment to the growth of others, and building community" (Greenleaf et al., 1996, pp. 3–7).

Listening

Both Piaget and Vygotsky were excellent listeners. Piaget was able to identify with what the children told him in Paris to discover learning mistakes. Vygotsky was an excellent listener who could also clarify the will of the group (Dobkin, 1982). Both could get in touch with their own inner voice and seek to understand what one's mind is communicating. Listening, coupled with regular periods of reflection, was essential to the formulation of their pedagogies.

Empathy

Both Piaget and Vygotsky were able to walk in the shoes of another. That is the heart of empathy. They were able to understand others and how they learned. When they both headed up research, they assumed the good intentions of their coworkers and did not reject them as people. This is true even when Vygotsky found out that Luria and Leont'ev had betrayed him. This is true even when Piaget discovered that his mentor Dr. Raymond was against Piaget investigating psychoanalysis, which Piaget was investigating to find a cure for his mother.

Healing

Healing is a powerful force for transformation and integration. Both Piaget and Vygotsky recognized that there were many other people who had suffered broken spirits and emotional hurts. Piaget and Vygotsky did not invent genetic epistemology and cultural–historical theory to just heal themselves personally nor get personal honor and glory. I believe that they developed their pedagogies in order to help others too. To help is to heal. Thus, both Piaget and Vygotsky recognized that they had an opportunity to make people/society whole and they took it.

Awareness

In general, awareness of others and oneself helps and strengthens a servant-leader. Piaget and Vygotsky could do this because they understood the issues involving ethics and values. In fact, their theories were partly written to combat the empiricists, Gestaltists, and behaviorists whose theories both Piaget and Vygotsky saw as harmful. Despite Piaget's mental breakdowns and despite Vygotsky's struggle with tuberculosis, both were able to have their own inner serenity. Vygotsky even stood up to Stalin indirectly by maintaining contact with the West, because he thought that Stalin was unethical. From the time he wrote *The Mission of the Idea* and *Reschere,* Piaget was a revolutionary; that is, he became determined to revolutionize epistemology. Both were aware of the problems within their societies and tried to deal with those problems so that their societies could become better.

Persuasion

Another characteristic of both Piaget and Vygotsky was their reliance on persuasion. Both were excellent speakers and authors. Rather than using their positional authority once they obtained their professional careers, they worked effectively at building consensus within their groups. Vygotsky first set up the Moscow troika and then set up ZPDs all over Moscow for his students and other colleagues. Piaget would retire to the mountains. He returned at the end of summer with a selection of topics for his group to research. He and his colleagues then would decide which topics they would research and how. Each researcher then worked independently of Piaget's supervision and control.

Conceptualization

Both Piaget and Vygotsky were masters at conceptualization. They had the ability to look at a problem from a conceptualizing perspective. They could think beyond the day-to-day realities of their situation. They had a sense of the past and a vision for the future. This ability allowed both men to create pedagogies from numerous concepts that were proved by their research.

Foresight

Foresight is similar to conceptualization. It means the ability to foresee the likely outcome of a situation or idea. Piaget and Vygotsky not only could understand the lessons of the past (especially, personal ones) they could also see the realities of the present and the likely consequence of a decision for the future. This is why Vygotsky tried to smuggle his work to the West during Stalin's reign. This is why Piaget decided to work for the United Nations. "The common wealth of all civilizations is the education of the child" (Piaget, 1940, p. 12). Foresight is deeply rooted within the intuitive mind. "As such…[it] is the one servant-leader characteristic with which one may be born. All other characteristics can be consciously developed" (Greenleaf et al.,1996, p. 5).

Stewardship

Stewardship means a commitment to the needs of others. It also empha-sizes the use of openness and persuasion rather than control (Greenleaf et al., 1996). Piaget showed stewardship throughout his professional career but the seeds of that virtue sprouted when he tried to understand while working among Parisian children who had trouble learning as he helped develop the intelligence test. He further exhibited this virtue when he worked at the Jean-Jacques Rousseau Institute. There, Piaget put his ideas into concrete operations and found them correct. Vygotsky showed stew-ardship throughout his life from childhood until his death in 1934. Every time Vygotsky set up a ZPD, every time he helped someone at risk to him-self (like when he nursed his dying brother Dodik), Vygotsky was showing stewardship.

Commitment to the Growth of Others

Both Piaget and Vygotsky committed themselves to the growth of peo-ple. Otherwise, they would never have spent their whole lives working on their pedagogies. For Vygotsky, the task hastened his death. I believe that one is never more committed to the good of others than one sacrifices for them. At his Swiss institutes, Piaget constantly recognized his responsibility to do everything within his power to nurture the personal and professional growth of his colleges (Piaget, 1980). This included making funds available for professional development, taking a personal interest in ideas and sug-gestions from everyone, encouraging worker involvement in decision mak-ing, and actively assisting workers with other problems (Piaget, 1976).

Building a Community

Finally, one of the first things that both Piaget and Vygotsky did when starting their professional careers was to build community. Although jun-ior to everyone at Kornilov's psychological institute, Vygotsky built a viable research community there very rapidly. He soon was made chief of the department (Luria, 1979). In Geneva, Piaget was also constantly working to create a viable research institute by giving everyone there a chance at research and publishing.

Conclusion

This biographical comparison between Jean Piaget and Lev Vygotsky has revealed many similarities between their personal life experiences. These similarities have shed light on the similarities of their ideas. Teachers can use these ideas to effectively teach their students the required subject matter. However, if teachers consider it their responsibility to educate the whole child, then teachers need to empower their students. How to do this empowering is observable by looking at the personal lives of Jean Piaget and Lev Vygotsky. Their comparative biographies reveal comparative virtues. These virtues made both Piaget and Vygotsky leaders in their field. If teachers want to follow in the footsteps of these two great men, they will empower their students with such virtues. For answers on how to best prepare students for leadership in the 21st century, teachers need to look not just at the ideas of Jean Piaget and Lev Vygotsky, but also at their biographies.

Corrie ten Bloom once wrote in her book, *The Hiding Place*, that someone came to her complaining about life. Corrie showed the young lady the needlework that Corrie had just finished. On the back, it looked like a mess of knots, twists, and tangled threads. On the front, it was a beautiful tapestry. Thus, all the difficulties that Piaget and Vygotsky endured were "stitched" by their six pillars (influences) into a beautiful pedagogy, designed to help others. I believe that genetic epistemology and cultural–historical theory would not have been created if both Piaget and Vygotsky had not had both encountered adversity and developed ideas to conquer the adversity.

However, all these small threads (i.e., influences) were needed to make the complete tapestry. Sometimes people, especially teachers, think that they have not done much good for others. Perhaps, they have done more good than they know, but in little ways. Maybe history is shaped not just by those who do great things but also by the preponderance of those who do the small things in life. Perhaps, genetic epistemology and cultural–historical theory are more a product of the constant, little influences in the lives of Piaget and Vygotsky than the major ones.

Techniques that Piaget and Vygotsky used can be adapted to today's classroom needs, especially since teachers today are being called to do more than just teach. Today's teacher is called upon to be a surrogate parent. Knowing genetic epistemology and cultural–historical theory will help the teacher teach, but knowing how Piaget and Vygotsky became follower-leaders will help that teacher be an effective guide.

In addition, educational philosophies become more vivid through the use of historical studies because they show the humanity behind the theories. Knowing more about how a theory was conceived advances the foundations of education and provides pedagogy with enlightenment.

Pedagogical ideas are not only the product of research but also the product of the theory maker. Jean Piaget and Lev Vygotsky existed in a historical context and it is that context that explains the origins of their ideas. Individuals bring to their work not only their research but also what makes them unique; that is, each person is a product of his heritage, time, environment, family, country, upbringing, education, and problems encountered in his life. In summation, both Piaget and Vygotsky were products of the milieu that shaped their research and developed within them a germinal image that started their contribution to humanity.

"Clearly, the motivational and cognitive origins of achievement are open to inquiry; their antecedents are rooted in family history, in social and cultural conditions, and in the specific events of a person's life" (John-Steiner, 1985, p. 35). The study of theory should not be divorced from the study of the theory maker. Biographical perspective adds muscle and skin to the otherwise dry bones of theory, and breathes humanity into the ideas of those who shape our learning.

CHAPTER 7

THE PEDAGOGY IF PIAGET
AND VYGOTSKY WERE ABLE
TO FULLY COLLABORATE

PREMISE

Many educators see the works of Jean Piaget and Lev Vygotsky as exact opposites when it comes to their lesson theories. Jean Piaget, it is argued, focused on the primacy of the individual in his genetic epistemology learning theory. On the other hand many believe that Lev Vygotsky focused on the social aspects of learning in cultural–historical theory.

"Vygotsky's ideas for bringing the importance of the social context in learning appear to be antinomious to those of Jean Piaget, who focused on individualization of learning" (Cole & Wertsch, 1996, p. 33). For Vygotsky, human inquiry is embedded within culture, which is embedded within social history (Glassman, 2001). For Piaget, human inquiry is embedded within the individual child, who constructs knowledge through his/her actions in the environment (Cole & Wertsch, 1996). This is how most students of an introduction to educational psychology course are taught and, perhaps, that was done because that might be the easiest way to break college freshmen into two complex theories. Anyway, that is how I remember my first educational psychology course being taught.

However, the more I studied the works and lives of Piaget and Vygotsky, the more I discovered that many of their ideas were complimentary. In this

Parallel Paths to Constructivism: Jean Piaget and Lev Vygotsky, pages 103–117
Copyright © 2004 by Information Age Publishing

chapter, I cite researchers who agree with me. Over time, I made historical inquiries into the origin of their ideas and discovered that both men did spend time communicating with one another. Every time they did communicate, they changed their ideas—mainly, to come more into agreement with each other. Unfortunately, Stalin effectively cut off all east–west communications by 1929. This action stymied but did not completely cut off their communicative attempts. Continuing to smuggle his work to the West, Vygotsky was put on trial by Stalin for "corrupting" Soviet thought with Western influences (Kozulin, 1991, p. 247). Vygotsky died of tuberculosis while working on his defense for this purge trial.

POINT OF VIEW

It is true that other researchers influenced Piaget and Vygotsky after both men started their professional careers in 1924 (Cole, 1984; Forman, 2003; Kozulin, 1991; Kozyrev & Turko, 1935; Leontiev, 1975; Montangero & Maurice-Naville, 1997; Prawat, 2002; Valsiner, 1998; Vygotsky, leter to Bozhovich, Levina, Morozova, Slavina, & Zaporozhec, 1929; Wertsch & Tulviste, 1992). This chapter is not concerned with the influence of others upon genetic epistemology and cultural–historical theory. This work is only concerned with how Piaget and Vygotsky influenced each other. The question is, should historical inquiry be stretched to allow for such an inquiry; namely, the possibility of a combined Piaget/Vygotsky pedagogy?

RATIONALE

The work of Russian psychologist L.S. Vygotsky has had a growing impact on education in America (Glassman, 2001). One might argue that the work of Swiss psychologist Jean Piaget has had an even more significant impact on American education (Van der Goot, 1989; Vidal, 1994). This research proposes that pedagogical ideas are not only the product of research but also the product of all the personal influences that affect a researcher's thinking. Using historical inquiry, this work proposes that both Jean Piaget and Lev Vygotsky tried to communicate their ideas to one another. This limited communication did influence these educational scholars to change their ideas in light of what the other communicated to them.

Historical inquiry "qualifies as a scientific endeavor from the same standpoint of its subscription to the same principles and the same general scholarship that characterizes all scientific research" (Cohen & Manion, 1989, p. 48). Indeed, in their writings, several authorities agree on the acceptability of history as a medium of scholarship (Cohen & Manion, 1989; Fraenkel & Wallen, 1990; Gall, Borg, & Gall, 1996; Gardiner, 1978).

It is possible to find solutions to contemporary problems (viz., how to best educate in this 21st century) by looking into the past (Cohen & Manion, 1989; Fraenkel & Wallen, 1990; Gall, Borg, & Gall, 1996; Hill & Kebert, 1967).

Modes of Inquiry

For clarification, this chapter is divided into four parts:

1. The attempts both Piaget and Vygotsky made to communicate with each other and how this influenced their learning theory ideas.
2. The methodology of this historical inquiry that is based on these communication attempts.
3. A proposal of what Piaget and Vygotsky's 12-point combined learning theory would have looked like should they have been fully able to exchange ideas.
4. A conclusion concerning the results of this historical inquiry.

Attempts at Communication

Both men tried to communicate their ideas to one another and, for about 5 years, that communication was active and effective. In 1924, after reading Piaget's book *Judgment and Reasoning of the Child*, Vygotsky wrote Piaget that learning was a sociocultural–historical event and sent him a copy of his 1923 book (Vygtosky, 1924 letter to Piaget). The result was that Piaget acknowledged the social aspects of learning. "There are no more such things as societies qua beings than there are isolated individuals" (Piaget, 1932, p. 360). Lenin died in 1924. Stalin started coming to power immediately and, as he consolidated dictatorial rule, started cutting off east–west communications—but at first this was only partially effective.

Stalin did not have complete dictatorial control until 1929. In 1926, Vygotsky was asked and agreed to write the preface for Piaget's Russian edition of his 1923 *Language and Thought of the Child* and also Piaget's 1924 book *Judgment and Reasoning of the Child*. A result of this work was that Piaget contributed the idea of four stages of epistemological development in humans to Vygotsky (1926). In other words, while already working on stages of human cognitive development, Vygotsky changed from three to four stages after reading Piaget, but refused to give them chronological settings, like Piaget had done (Vygotsky, 1926).

In 1926, Piaget wrote in the Foreword of that Russian translation (second edition) of his 1923 *Language and Thought of the Child* that he welcomed collaboration with Soviet psychologists. Vygotsky then sent his 1926 work, *Psychological Pedagogy*, to Piaget. Piaget would not receive that work until 1934 because of Stalin's effectiveness in cutting off east–west communications. However, when he received that work, Piaget changed some of his learning theory. In his second edition of *Language and Thought of the Child*, Piaget admitted in his new Foreword that there was a possibility that a child's learning might be impacted socially (Newman & Holzman, 1993).

Vygotsky made repeated attempts after that to have his work taken out of the USSR to Piaget, but became quickly frustrated due to growing Stalinist repression and censorship of the mails (Newman & Holzman, 1993). Vygotsky did send his 1926 *Psychological Pedagogy* to Piaget in 1927. Unfortunately, Piaget would not get this manuscript until 1932 because Stalin had become more effective in cutting off communication. Piaget's response was to concede in his next work, *Moral Judgment of the Child*, that there is a historical context for some reasoning (Piaget, 1932).

In the early 1960s, Piaget was finally able to read a book that Vygotsky wrote and tried to send to Piaget in 1932 entitled *Thinking and Speech*. Prior to 1964, Piaget only had a role for external speech (talking). However, after reading Vygotsky's work, Piaget then wrote a commentary on it stating the value of internal speech (Piaget, 1962). "If you go back and look closely at *Language and Thought of the Child*, you will see that Piaget hovers over the issue of individual/social and takes the individual path while recognizing that it is not the only way to go" (M. Cole, personal communication, May 15, 2003).

For the first and only time, Vygotsky left the USSR in 1925 to speak at a conference on defectology and educating the deaf in London. Piaget was at that conference but did not attend Vygotsky's lecture. In 1929, Piaget addressed two major conventions in America to which Vygotsky could only send a paper via his colleague Luria. At the second convention (Ninth International Psychological Congress) in New Haven, Connecticut, Luria spoke with Piaget (M. Berrar, email of 2/18/04 to Pass). Nothing is recorded of what transpired but the result was that Piaget would agree with Vygotsky's premise (subject of the paper would evolve into a 1930 book entitled "Ape, Primitive Man, and Child") that not all people reach the top stage of cognitive development (Vygotsky and Luria, 1930; Piaget, 1957).

One result of this inability to adequately communicate in a timely fashion due to Stalin's repression was that Vygotsky rejected Piaget's idea that the learner, not the teacher, interacting with the environment was the only thing necessary for new constructs to emerge. In 1933, the local government around both Neuchatel and Geneva, where Piaget was working, became "obsessively anticommunist" (Vidal, 1989, p. 103). Piaget, unable to hear from Vygotsky but aware of the violence of Stalin's dictatorship, would stop his teachers from speaking in the classroom unless it was to ask diagnostic questions because he was concerned about indoctrination (N.R. Colet, personal communication, March 15, 2001).

Writing from Moscow after the fall of communism, Alexander Kozulin noted in his 1991 work that it was the influence of both communism and westerners like Piaget that developed Vygotsky's cultural–historical theory. This influence was especially true when Stalin began his purges in the mid-1930s. Vygotsky, trying to stay alive, worked on the idea that learning was an activity but was unable to have any of his work published (Kozulin, 1991). Kozulin hinted that Stalin probably repressed Vygotsky's work because Vygotsky's idea that learning was an activity was just as much Piagetian as it was Marxist. Kozulin wrote that Stalin wanted to purge Soviet thought from "corrupting" Western influences. Kozulin was the first to write that Leontiev adapted Vygotsky's idea to coincide with what Stalin wanted and became famous for it "as a response to immediate political circumstances" (1991, p. 247). In the 1960s, as Soviet repression lessened, Leontiev would recant his betrayal and start promoting Vygotsky's ideas—including to Westerners.

METHODOLOGY

The four steps used by this study for its historical communication of ideas were: (1) identifying the topic, (2) searching for relevant information, (3) evaluating the information, and (4) synthesizing the historical facts into a meaningful interpretation that can shed light on present and future trends. Such a methodology is valid for historical research (Cohen & Manion, 1989; Fraenkel & Wallen, 1990; Gall, Borg, & Gall, 1996; Hill & Kebert, 1967).

Electronic data was used in this investigation. The computer-enabled access into the archives of the Russian Academy of Science, Moscow State University, and the Piaget archives at the University of Geneva. From there, I "webbed out" by investigating sources cited in those archives. This enabled me to gain e-mail access to various authorities (including Leontiev's son and Vygotsky's daughter). In addition, secondary sources available at local libraries were also read. From there, I webbed out from the bibliographies of what I read to other sources of information. This work took approximately five years.

COMBINED PEDAGOGY

Using the above methodology, I looked at the major ideas that formulate genetic epistemology and cultural–historical theory and concluded that a Piaget–Vygotsky pedagogy would consist of the following 12 ideas:

1. Both would focus on the individual within the group (e.g., where there is an individual assignment/grade within a group assignment/grade).

2. Piaget would agree to a more active role for the teacher. The teacher would brief before and after a lesson, but let the child create a mental construct by himself/herself to solve the lesson (Tudge and Winterhoff, 1993). This would be done in a group setting with both group grades/assignments and individual grades/assignments.

3. Both would have the student use inquiry-based instruction. The teacher is there to instruct before and debrief after the lesson but the student solves the problem.

4. Both would have external (talking) and internal language (thinking to oneself) as a tool of learning.

5. Both would have stages of development. Vygotsky would use Piaget's terms and Piaget would agree not to set specific ages for the stages.

6. Both would agree to a rich learning environment correctly set at the child's stage of development.

7. Both would agree to construct formation whereby a child constructs a mental model to solve the problem but this could be done as an individual within a group.

8. "Piaget's equilibration is similar to Vygotsky's idea of internalization." (Steffe, 1995, p. 510). I believe that Vygotsky would agree to Piaget's term.

9. Vygotsky would be able to persuade Piaget that unstructured play includes learning.

10. Piaget would be able to persuade Vygotsky that error is acceptable and a child can learn from it. However, they recommend that lessons be set to the correct stage of development so that the child has a reasonable chance of success.

11. Both would agree that not all could reach the highest stage of development. Piaget would say it was because the learning environment was not correctly set to the stage of development and Vygotsky would say that it was because of the fault of the social milieu.

12. Both would agree to the concepts of optimal mismatch and scaffolding (explained earlier).

The Individual within the Group

For Vygotsky, human inquiry is embedded within culture, which is embedded within social history. The educational process works, more or less, from the outside in. In contrast, Piaget emphasizes individual human inquiry" (Glassman, 2001, p. 3). As Michael Cole and James Wertsch cite (Smith, 1995), Piaget did not deny the coequal role of the social world in the construction of knowledge. "There is no longer any need to choose between the primacy of the social or that of the intellect" (Piaget, 1970, p. 114). "If you go back and look closely at *Language and Thought of the Child,* you will see that Piaget hovers over the issue of individual/social and takes the individual path while recognizing that it is not the only way to go" (Cole, 2003).

Vygotsky, contrary to stereotypical knowledge, also insisted on the centrality of active construction of knowledge (Cole & Wertsch, 1996). "But we have seen that where the child's egocentric speech is linked to his practical activity, where it is linked to his thinking, things really do operate on his mind and influence it. By the word "things," we mean reality...as it is encountered in practice" (Vygotsky, 1987, pp. 78–79).

My research indicated that these two men would have agreed on social individualism in learning; that is, a child constructs a mental model to solve the problem by himself/herself but can be aided in this process through the intervention of a "social other." This can be done by assignment of individual tasks with accompanying individual grades within a group assignment with a group grade. Kagan (2003) has already started this method in America and it was used by my high school that went from unacceptable ratings of student academic achievement to acceptable to recommended in 3 years (this is considered a significant accomplishment).

Role of the Teacher

Piaget, unlike Vygotsky, was never a classroom teacher but he was a diagnostician for many years in Paris and Geneva. Furthermore, Piaget's experience at his elementary school, the Latin School, was less than happy. He got high marks but his classroom teachers did not give him a happy, nurturing education (Barrelet & Perret-Clermont, 1996). In fact, Piaget wrote a book about teachers in 1954 that was so scathing, it has yet to be published in English. In his autobiography, Piaget (1952) further paints a less-than-acceptable teacher/school experience.

With his work both in Paris and later, at the Jean-Jacques Rousseau Institute, Piaget confirmed the idea set in his childhood at the Latin School that the teacher should only function as a diagnostician—not an active instructor. Furthermore, unlike the impoverished USSR, Piaget's Switzerland was prosperous enough to enable a teacher to provide an intellectually stimulating classroom environment. Vygotsky had to rely on a cheaper method of instruction; namely, paying a teacher to use language to scaffold a child up to the height of that child's zone of proximal development

(ZPD), which is the difference between the knowledge the child can obtain on her/his own and the knowledge that the child can obtain with the help of a "social other" (Gredler, 1997; Vygotsky, 1934/1984).

However, Piaget would still have focused on the individual and Vygotsky the social but could have combined them by having the teacher brief (short lecture) before and after the lesson. The teacher would have set the learning environment at the child's chronological stage of development for Piaget or ZPD for Vygotsky. Piaget believed that learning was set within the limits of chronological age and Vygotsky believed that learning could be seen as the ZPD or range between what one can learn by oneself and what one can learn with the help of a knowledgeable "social other." This "social other" does not always have to be a teacher.

Inquiry-Based Instruction

Both Piaget and Vygotsky were advocates of inquiry-based instruction. This is defined as the student perceiving the problem, constructing a mental model to solve the problem, and then forming a solution. Piaget's free and individual inquiry is different from the culturally social inquiry of Vygotsky (Glassman, 2001; Vygotsky, 1987). Both, however, believe in constructivism. The heart of constructivism in education is critical thinking (Leonard, 2003). Constructivist lessons are often described as student-led learning where the teacher debriefs before and after but sets up a learning situation where the students discover the solution him- or herself (Leonard, 2003).

Piaget and Vygotsky differ most on the role of the teacher (Kuhn, 1979). Piaget initially rejected Vygotsky's idea of the "social other" because throughout Piaget's childhood and adolescence, anyone assigned by Piaget's society to nurture and educate him failed to do so. Vygotsky, on the other hand, experienced his "social others" not only educating him but also saving his life during pogroms and preparing him successfully for a difficult task, a Jew receiving admission to the Imperial University of Moscow during the reign of the last Czar. Vygotsky's idea of the "social other" resulted from personal experiences that took place by all people assigned by his society to nurture and educate him. This would include Vygotsky's parents, siblings, friends, hometown, education, and the Jewish culture.

I believe that both Piaget and Vygotsky would acknowledge the role of the social in learning. "…[A] particular social environment remains indispensible for the realization of [the possibilities accorded by the maturation of the nervous system]" (Inhelder and Piaget, 1995, p. 337). Moreover, Piaget wrote that the teacher–child interaction is useful "…to the extent that the intelligent teacher [is able] to efface himself or herself, to become an equal and not a superior, to discuss and to examine, rather than to agree and constrain morally" (Piaget and Inhelds, 1969, p. 231). Thus, in a combined Piaget–Vygotsky pedagogy, the teacher would be a facilitator rather than a dictator of learning.

Stages of Development

Piaget wrote that there were four chronological stages of reasoning development: sensorimotor, birth to $1^1/_2$ years; preoperational, from 2–3 to 7–8 years; concrete operational, 7–8 to 12–14 years; and formal operational (older than 14 years) (Gredler, 1997). For Vygotsky, it was his interest in literature and its analysis that created the idea in Vygotsky's mind of stages of development (Dobkin, 1982). While working at the Neuchatel Museum of Natural History as a youth, Piaget developed the idea of chronological stages of development while watching the mollusks and snails react in the lab. Later, he was influenced by the works of Darwin, Bergson, Sabatier, and Reymond to explore how their ideas fit with his observations of development (Peterman, 1997). It was while he was working at the Binet lab in Paris and with Pierre Janet in Paris that Piaget was finally able to write down the concept of chronological stages of development. Still later, while working at the Rousseau Institute in Geneva and observing in its activity school, Piaget would be able to do research to prove that this idea was valid.

What Piaget wanted to do was to cleanse epistemology of the irrational and he wanted to discover an evolution of cognitive development much like Darwin did for the biological. Vygotsky may have used decentration as a means to trace the evolution of the basis of knowledge from the primitive to the advanced (Peterman, 1997). So, Piaget did have a sense of the historical when he developed this idea of chronological stages of development.

Piaget was to write two books, *Language and Thought of the Child* in 1923 and *Judgment and Reasoning in the Child* in 1924, that would motivate Vygotsky to publish his own stages of development; namely, precausality, secondary differentiation, and differentiation (Vygotsky, 1929).

After reading Piaget and writing the Russian translation of the introduction to Piaget's *Language and Thought of the Child*, Vygotsky divided his first stage of precausality into two parts. In short, Vygotsky's precausality became primary differentiation and real instrumental. Now, Vygotsky had four stages of development: primary differentiation, real instrumental, secondary differentiation, and differentation (Kozulin, 1991). However, Vygotsky refused to set chronological age limits to his stages of development and also acknowledged that some societies might never reach the highest stage (Wertsch, 1985) due to their primitiveness. Piaget would later agree with that not all people will reach the final stage of development.

Dobkin, Vygotsky's childhood friend, wrote that it was Vygotsky's work in literary analysis that started Vygotsky into formulating his stages of development (Dobkin, 1982).

Therefore, both Piaget and Vygotsky would have agreed to the idea of stages of development and I believe that Vygotsky would use Piaget's own childhood activity to prove that these do not have to be set to chronological age—Piaget wrote his first booklet on an auto vamp (invented car) when he was eight and a book, *Un Moineau Albinos*, when he was 10 that was so well written that he was offered a curator's job at another Swiss museum of natural history (Bringuier, 1980).

Language

> Commentators on the differences between these two thinkers [Piaget and Vygotsky] have placed too narrow an emphasis on their ideas regarding the primary of individual psychogenesis versus sociogenesis of mind, while neglecting what we believe is a cardinal difference between them: their views concerning the importance of culture—in particular the mediation of action through artifacts—in the development of mind. (Cole & Wertsch, 1996, p. 34)

Artifacts are tools. It is the artifact as an educational tool that gives meaning to the lesson. Tools are defined as "a malleable set of means" (Glassman, 2001), such as language.

Neither Piaget (1923) nor Vygotsky (1934/1984; see also Introduction to Russian translation of Piaget's 1923 work in 1926) ignored the importance of language in learning, although Piaget did not consider it as the educational equivalent of Marx's dialectic. I believe that, had he and Vygotsky been able to communicate, Piaget would have accepted most of Vygotsky's more active view of artifacts, although Piaget would not have embraced the dialectical materialism concept to which Vygotsky attributed language (Vygotsky, 1987).

Vygotsky and Piaget both had a role for language in education (Luria, 1979; Yaroshevsky, 1996). Piaget believed that social interaction was not as important as inner speech (Davydov & Radzikhovsky, 1985). Although he also believed that the use of language during instruction can show a lack of operative thinking (Piaget, 1962). Piaget accepted the idea that the teacher could use language as a way to diagnose the correct classroom learning environment from his experiences; first, in Paris working on Simon and Binet's test and, second, in Geneva working for the Jean-Jacques Rousseau Institute.

Nevertheless, Piaget would initially reject Vygotsky's stronger role for language as a tool of instruction because it showed a lack, in Piaget's opinion, of operative thinking (Piaget, 1962). "Piaget's reluctance to view language as one of the good things of development goes back to his early suspicion that it is the language of adult constraint which confines the child within himself" (Modgil, Modgil & Brown, 1983, p. 91) and could make it possible for a dictatorial government to control a child's mind. However, Vygotsky's egocentric speech is very content oriented, and he wrote that the content of language is critical to leading a child to newer and better constructs (Davydov & Radzkowvsky, 1985). Joining Hegel with his own personal experiences, Vygotsky formalized in Gomel after his return from Kiev that communication was the tool of learning. Because he saw Lenin as liberating, Vygotsky wanted to prove Karl Marx correct (Newman & Holzman, 1993) and wrote that language was a tool of learning to endorse Marx's theory of dialectical materialism.

After Vygotsky wrote *Myshelenie i rech* (*Thinking and Speech*) in 1932, he tried to get it to Piaget (Lenin died in 1924 and by 1927 Stalin had almost complete dictatorial control over the USSR). Piaget did not read it until 1962. After reading it, Piaget wrote a commentary in which he acknowledged the importance of internal speech (thinking to oneself) (Piaget, 1962). In conclusion, both Piaget and Vygotsky would accept a role for internal and external language as a tool of instruction. Piaget would initially reject, however, Vygotsky's value of egocentric speech (babbling) because Piaget would fear it could indicate or lead to mental illness—Piaget had at least two institutionalizations for mental breakdowns (Vidal, 1994) and Piaget's father hospitalized his mother for 3 months for mental instability (Piaget, 1952). However, since Vygotsky's egocentric speech is very content orientated and Vygotsky wrote that the content of language is critical to leading a child to newer and better constructs (Darydov and Radzkowsky, 1985), Piaget would have accepted a role for egocentric speech.

Learning Environment

Vygotsky wrote and thought at a time when his country had little resources to provide a rich learning environment for students. Piaget, on the other hand, was a product of Switzerland and that country could afford such an environment. Both Piaget and Vygotsky corresponded with Montessori (Vygotsky, 1929) and Dewey (Glassman, 2001). Had he lived, I believe that Vygotsky would agree with Piaget on having a rich learning environment correctly set to the child's stage of development.

Equilibration and Internalization

Equilibration is a set of processes that coordinate cognitive development in the individual's search for "true" equilibrium (Gredler, 1997). "Equilibration is similar to Vygotsky's idea of internalization" (Steffe and Gale, 1995, p. 510; Hamilton, 1997). Vygotsky termed internalization to describe the processes of cognitive development that a person goes though to understand something (Gredler, 1997). Piaget developed this idea while in the Swiss mountains recuperating from two mental breakdowns. This idea was endorsed by the philosophers introduced to him by his father, godfather, and own personal readings. He was able to formalize this idea in his mind when he both worked and studied in Paris (Kesselring, 1988). The final confirmation came when he worked at the Jean-Jacques Rousseau Institute, where he was able to test his idea in a controlled classroom environment (N.R. Colet, personal communication, March 15, 1999).

Vygotsky's idea of internalization was born during his family's ZPDs around the family samovar in the dining room during the long Russian winters. It developed during the literary sessions that transpired as childhood play with his friends and siblings. His first tutor, Solomon Aspiz, successfully used this method to train Vygotsky so that when he entered his private Jewish gymnasium for only 2 years of education, he was able to obtain the gold medal given for the best scholar. In addition, the philosophies of Hegel, introduced by Vygotsky's father to him, and the Gestalt psychologists, which he studied after graduating from his two universities, also endorsed this idea. Internalization was further formalized as a teacher in Gomel (both in the classroom and in his psychological laboratory that he set up there). However, it was endorsed after Vygotsky read Piaget's book, *Le Judgement et le Raisonment Chez Infant*. Finally, Vygotsky also read Bergson and Darwin. Those two authors further endorsed Vygotsky's idea of internalization. Both Piaget and Vygotsky agreed on this concept and would include it in their combined learning theory.

Play

Piaget saw play as only acceptable as an early life experience (babyhood), and believed that it was a waste of time after that stage of development. It was unstructured thinking, and that could lead to madness (Piaget, 1962, 1966). For Piaget, with the development of symbolic play, the child increasingly goes beyond single status faction of manipulating reality (Nicolopoulou, 1993) and individual processes to social play and collective symbolism (Nicolopoulou, 1993). Vygotsky, on the other hand, because of his personal experiences while growing up in Gomel with his family, friends, and hometown's ZPDs, believed that play was a great learning experience. Vygotsky's childhood play was a valuable learning experience (Vygotsky, 1967). I think that Vygotsky could have used Piaget's experience at Switzerland's "activity schools" plus Montessori (with whom they both communicated) to convince Piaget that play includes learning. Thus, their combined learning theory would have included play for children's learning.

Error

Vygotsky saw error as something to be avoided, and Piaget saw it as part of the learning process (Forman, 1980). In scientific experiments, error is an acceptable outcome. Often, it is as important to prove something incorrect as to prove it correct. It is not considered a failure if the positive hypothesis is proven incorrect through objective, scientific investigation. Therefore, Piaget, who used science to form a rational epistemology, would evolve the idea that error is allowable. Piaget reasoned that failure in life or education is not to be avoided. One can perhaps learn more from one's mistakes than one's accomplishments. He learned this when his father rejected Piaget's idea of the "auto vap" at age 8 and his first book, *Our Birds,* a year later. The result was that Piaget tried harder and, when only 10, his *Un Moineu Albinos* was published as an adult work. Piaget's idea was confirmed, however, not only in his life experiences, but also with his work both in Paris and Geneva. By the time Piaget became a professor of psychology, sociology, and the philosophy of science at the University of Neuchatel in 1925, this idea was in place.

On a personal note, Piaget's own hospitalizations demonstrated to him that conflict was essential for growth. Without his first nervous breakdown in 1915, he would not have accepted the attempt to purify philosophy, through the use of science, of its irrational factors (Sants, 1994). Without his second nervous breakdown starting in 1917, perhaps he would not have discovered the ideas of equilibration and accommodation. Thus, to Piaget error or conflict was part of life's processes and could result in better ideas.

Vygotsky wrote that error or failure occurs when the social other is not doing a correct, nurturing job; that is, incorrectly passing on the solutions that the student's society has found over time (Vygotsky, 1967). In Vygotsky's country, making mistakes could get you killed (Dobkin, 1982). The persecutions, pogroms, wars, and purges did not leave much room for error. So, while Piaget could accept the concept of error because Switzerland was a peaceful, democratic country and because the scientific research process (that Piaget engaged often in) accepted it, Vygotsky could not. Furthermore, Piaget's two hospitalizations proved to him that error, or conflict, was essential for intellectual growth, but Vygotsky's own experience with two pogroms while still a child and his own father's trial for defending his family, convinced him at an early age that error was to be avoided (Forman, 1980). Finally, Marx did not provide for error, and if Vygotsky was going to prove Marxism correct, he also could not provide for error.

Had Vygotsky not died in 1934, with the fall of communism in Russia, Piaget would have been able to convince Vygotsky that error would be acceptable in the classroom. In return, Piaget would have compromised by getting the teacher or "social other" to lead the student to the reason for the mistake and let the student try again with that knowledge.

Optimal Mismatch and Scaffolding

Scaffolding is very "similar to Piaget's idea of the optimal mismatch" (Kuhn, 1979, p. 356). In Piaget's idea of the optimal mismatch, a classroom environment is set at the highest challenging point for a student's chronological stage of development so that, with effort, a child can move, if the child successfully internalizes the problem, through equilibration to the top of that child's stage of development (Hamilton, 1997).

Piaget's optimal mismatch corresponds to Vygotsky's idea of "scaffolding" as explained by Jerome Bruner (Bruner, 1967; Kuhn, 1979). The optimal mismatch takes place when the challenge is placed at the top of the child's stage of chronological development. The tension that occurs from this demanding task results in the child rising higher intellectually by solving the difficult problem. Piaget first developed this idea while working in the Museum of Natural History in Neuchatel. However, this idea bloomed to fruition, first, in Paris with his investigations for Burt's test and, second, with his work at the Rousseau Institute. Piaget faced his own problems and solved them by using the optimal mismatch. The inner "angst" caused by his childhood family relationships did result in creativity—Piaget created genetic epistemology.

Scaffolding is a term that was not used by Vygotsky, even though Vygotsky conceptualized the idea. It was first used by Jerome Bruner (1967) to describe a student being brought from the bottom of his stage of development to the top by a caring "social other" through the use of communication. Bruner was one of the first authors to see the similarities between Piaget and Vygotsky.

In Piaget, a classroom environment is set at the highest challenging point for a student's chronological stage of development so that, with effort, a child can move through equilibration to the top of that child's stage of development, if the child successfully internalizes the problem (Hamilton, 1997).

For Vygotsky, this sociohistorical context of learning continues generation after generation to create a society whose learning is spiraling ever upward as one generation builds upon the learning of the other; thus, societies are scaffolding upward as well. Vygotsky developed this idea from a lifetime of experiences: his parents, his siblings, his cousins, his friends, his hometown, and his jobs. With his interest in the philosophers mentioned in this chapter, it was not difficult for Vygotsky to take those personal experiences and join them with Marx's philosophy of history—it neatly coincided with Vygotsky's idea on the role of communication in learning (Bruner, 1967). In conclusion, both Piaget and Vygotsky would have included optimal mismatch and scaffolding within their combined theories.

CONCLUSION

My comparison between Jean Piaget and Lev Vygotsky has revealed the impact on their ideas by their personal life experiences and the mutual communication showing how the exchange of those ideas influenced each other. When coupled with the changes that they made in their ideas as a result of communication, it is possible to list 12 ideas that they could have agreed on had their communication with each other not been curtailed by Stalin. This knowledge enhances the foundations of education and sheds light on the development of learning theory. I believe that effective teachers today are already utilizing a combined Piaget/Vygotsky pedagogy. I used such a method during my public high school teaching career and I also saw my colleagues using it. Nevertheless, should historical inquiry be stretched to formally write that such pedagogy exists?

BIBLIOGRAPHY

PRIMARY

Baldwin, J. M. (1894). *Mental development in the child and the race, methods and processes.* New York: Macmillan.

Bandura, A. (1986). *Social foundations of thought and action.* Englewood Cliffs, NJ: Prentice Hall.

Bergson, J. (1896). *Matiere et memoire: Essai sur la relation du corps a l'esprit* [Subject and matter: Test on the relation of the bodies of the spirit]. Paris: Vrin.

Bringuier, J. (1980). *Conversations with Jean Piaget.* Chicago: University of Chicago Press.

Bruner, J. (1967). *Contemporary approaches to cognition.* Cambridge, MA: Harvard University Press.

Claparede, E. (1917). La psychologie de l'inteligence. *Scientia, 22,* 353–368.

Cole, M., & Wertsch, J. (1996, September-October). Beyond the individual–social antimony in discussions of Piaget and Vygotsky. In D. Kuhn (Ed.), *Human development.* New York: Karger.

Darwin, C. (1859). *On the origin of species.* Cambridge. MA: Harvard University Press.

Davydov, V. (Ed.). (1982). *One is not born a personality.* Moscow: Progress.

Dobkin, S. (1982). Ages and days. In. K. Levitin, *One is not born a personality* (pp. 23–38). Moscow: Progress.

Ehrenburg, I. (1962). *Men, years, life.* Cleveland, OH: World.

Evans, R. (1922). *Dialogue with Jean Piaget.* New York: Praeger.

Glassman, M. (May 2001). Dewey and Vygotsky: Society, experience, and inquiry in educational practice. *Educational Researcher.* 30(4), 3–14.

Godet, P. (1901). *Neuchatel pittoresque. La ville et le vignoble.* Secheron-Geneve, Switzlerland: S.A. des Arts Graphiques.

Parallel Paths to Constructivism: Jean Piaget and Lev Vygotsky, pages 119–126
Copyright © 2004 by Information Age Publishing

Godet, P. (1904). *Palees et bondelles. RS, 38*, 25–27.

Godet, P. (1902). *La journee de Peseux. Musee Neuchatelois, 39*, 267–272.

Gredler, M. (1997). *Learning and instruction: Theory in to practice*. Upper Saddle River, NJ: Merrill.

Hall, E. (1970). A conversation with Jean Piaget and Barbel Inhelder. *Psychology Today, 3*, 25–32.

Inhelder, B. & Piaget, J. (1958). *The growth of logical thinking from childhood to adolescence*. NY: Basic Books.

James, W. (1909). *Pragmatism, a new name for some old ways of thinking*. London: Longmans, Green.

Janet, P. (1902). De l'emotion. Problems psychologiques les stades de l'evolution psychologique [The stages of psychological evolution]. *Revue Neurologique, 2*, 1551–1558.

Janet, P. (1914). Les tendances intellectueles relatives a la rescherche de la verite. *Annuaire du College de France, 14–15*, 80–91.

Kagan, S. (2003). *Notes from Spencer* [Online]. Available: www.KaganOnline.com.

Kornilov, K. N. (1922). *Uchenie o reakcijakj cheloveka s psikhologicheskoj tochki zrenija*. Moscow: Gosudarstvennoe Izatel'stvo.

Kozyrev, A., & Turko, P. (1935). Pedagogicheskaja shkola. professor L. Vygotskogo. *Vyshaja Shkola, 2*, 44–57.

Le Dantec, F. (1895). *La matiere vivante*. Paris: Masson.

Leontiev, A. N. (1975). *Djatel'nost' soznanie lichnost*. Moscow: Izdatel'stvo Politicheskoh Literatury.

Levitin, K. (1982) The Mozart of psychology. In V. Davydov (Ed.), *One is not born a personality*. Moscow: Progress.

Luria, A. R. (1979). *The making of mind: A personal account of Soviet psychology*. Cambridge, MA: Harvard University Press.

Luria, A. R. (1982). *Language and cognition*. New York: Wiley.

Mandel'shtam, N. (1920). *Tristia*. Moscow: Progress.

Mandel'shtam, N. (1970). *Vospominanija. Kinga Pervaja*. Paris: YMCA Press.

Mitjushin, A. A. (1988). I ego mesto v istorii otechestvennoj psikhologii. Vestnik Moskovskogo Universiteta. Serija 13. *Psikhologija, 2*, 33–42.

Piaget, J. (1912/1977). L'albinisme chez la Limnaea stagnalis In H. Gruber & Voneche (Eds. & Trans.), *The essential Piaget: An interpretive reference and guide*. New York: Basic Books.

Piaget, J. (1914). Bergson et Sabatier. *Revue chretienne, 61*, 19–22.

Piaget, J. (February 5, 1915). Letter to Paul Pettavel.

Piaget, J. (September 25, 1915). Letter to A. Reymond.

Piaget, J. (1915). *La Mission de l'Idee*. Lausanne: La Concorde.

Piaget, J. (October 5, 1918). Letter to A. Reymond.

Piaget, J. (1918/1980). *Recherches sur la Contradiction* [Research of the contradiction]. Lausanne: La Concorde.

Piaget, J. (1921). Introduction a la malacologie Valaisanne. *Bulletin de la Murithienne, 42*, 82–112.

Piaget, J. (1923). *Language and thought of the child*. Paris: Delachaux & Nestle.

Piaget J. (1924/1926). *Judgement and reasoning of the child*. Paris: Delachaux & Nestle.

Piaget J. (1932). *The moral judgment of the child*. London: Kegan Paul.

Piaget, J. (1945). *Play, dreams, and imitation in childhood*. London: Heinemann.

Piaget, J. (1952). Jean Piaget. In E. Boring, H. Langfeld, H. Werner, & R. Yerkes (Eds.), *A history of psychology in autobiography, IV*. Worcester, MA: Clark University Press.

Piaget, J. (1957). *Construction of reality in the child*. London: Routledge and Kegan Paul.

Piaget, J. (1959). An outline of intellectual autobiography. In *Insights and Illusions of Philosophy*. Geneva, Switzerland: University of Geneva Press.

Piaget, J. (1962). *Commentaire sur les remarquest critiques de Vygotski concernant le Langage et la pensee chez l'enfant et le Judgement et le raissonement chez l'enfant* [Commentary on the ideas of Vygotsky concerning language and the judgment of the child]. Boston: MIT Press.

Piaget, J. (1965). *Insights and illusions of philosophy* (H. Weaver, Trans.). New York: Basic Books.

Piaget J. (1966a). Autobiographie. *Cahiers Vilfredo Pareto (Revue europeene des sciences socials)*, *4*, 129–159.

Piaget, J. (1966b). Response to Brian Sutton-Smith. *Psychological Review, 73*, 111–112.

Piaget, J. & Inhelder, B. (1969). *The psychology of the child*. NY: Basic Books.

Piaget, J. (1970a). *Genetic epistemology*. New York: Columbia University Press.

Piaget, J. (1970b). *Science of education and the psychology of the child*. New York: Orion.

Piaget, J. (1970c). *Structuralism*. NY: Basic Books.

Piaget, J. (1973). *The child and reality: Problems of genetic psychology*. New York: Viking.

Piaget, J. (1976). Autobiographie. *Cahiers Vilfredo Pareto (Revue europeenne des sciences sociales)*, *14*, 1–43.

Piaget, J. (1980). *Conversations with Jean Piaget*. Chicago: University of Chicago Press.

Piaget, J. (1996, Fall). *Genetic epistemology* [Online]. Available: http://www.unige.ch/paiget/docug.html.

Piaget, R. (February 5, 1915). Letter to Paul Pettavel.

Piaget, R. (May 17, 1916). Letter to Paul Pettavel.

Preyer, W. (1882). *Die selle des kindes: beobachtung uber die geisteige entwicklung des menschen in den ersten levensj*ahren [Children's minds: observations of human mental development in the first years of life]. Leipzig, Germany: Grieben.

Rotman, B. (1977). *Jean Piaget: Psychologist of the real*. Brighton, UK: Harvester Press.

Shpet, G. (1927). *Vnutrennjaja forma slova*. Moscow: Gosudarstvennaja Akademija Khudozhestvennykh Nauk.

Spencer, J. (1855). *The principles of psychology*. London: Longman & Brown.

Van Biema, E. (1908). *L'espace et le temps chez Liebniz et chez Kant*. Paris: Alcan.

Vygodskaya, G. (January 1994/September 1996). *Remembering father*. Paper delivered to coommemorative seminar for Lev Vygotsky and redelivered at second conference for sociocultural research, Moscow/Geneva.

Vygodskaya, G. & Lifanova, T. (1996). *Lev Semenovich Vygotsky*. Moscow: Smysl.

Vygotsky, L. S. (1916). Review of A. Belyh. *Novyi put'*, *47*, 27–32.

Vygotsky, L. S. (1924, October). *The methodology of reflexology and psychological studies*. Paper presented to the Second Psychological Congress, Leningrad, USSR.

Vygotsky, L. S. (1924). Letter to Piaget.

Vygotsky, L. S. (March 5, 1926). Letter to A. K. Luria.

Vygotsky, L. S. (1926). Metodika refleksologicheskogo i psikhologicheskogo issle-dovanija. In K. N. Kornilov (Ed.), *Problemy sovremennoj psikhologii* (pp. 26–46). Leningrad: Gosudarstvennoe Izdatel'stvo.

Vygotsky, L. S. (1928). *Judgment and reasoning in the child.* Moscow: The Psychological Institute.

Vygotsky, L. S. (1929/1962). *Myshlenie i rech.* Moscow: Gosudarstvennoe Sotsial'no-Ekonomicheskoe Izdatel'stvo. (Reprinted and translated as *Thought and Language.* Cambridge, MA: MIT Press.).

Vygotsky, L. S. (April 15, 1929). Letter to Bozhovich, Levina, Morozorn, Slavina, and Zaporzhec.

Vygotsky, L. S. & Luria, A. R. (1930/1992). *Ape, primitive man, and child: Essays in the history of behavior.* (Trans. by E. Rossita). NY: Harvester.

Vygotsky, L. S. (1934/1978). *Mind in society: The development of higher psychological processes.* Cambridge, MA: Harvard University Press.

Vygotsky, L. S. (1967). Play and its role in the mental development of the child. *Soviet Psychology, V,* 3–17.

Vygotsky, L. S. (1925/1971). *The psychology of art* (Scripta Technica, Inc., Trans.). Cambridge, MA: MIT Press.

Vygotsky, L. S. (1984). *Solobranie sochinenii, tom4, detskaya psickholigiya* [Collected works, vol. 4., child psychology]. Moscow: Pedagogika.

Vygotsky, L. S. (1987). *The collected works of L. S. Vygotsky. Vol. 1 Problems of general psychology (including the volume "Thinking and Speech").* Trans. by N. Minick. NY: Plenum.

Vygotsky, L. S. (1934/1984) *Mind in society: The development of higher psychological processes* (M. Cole, V. John-Steiner, S. Scribner, & E. Souberman). Cambridge, MA: Harvard University Press.

Vygotsky, L.S. (1987). *The collected works of L. S. Vygotsky: Vol. 1. Problems of general psychology.* New York: Plenum Press.

Vygotsky, L. S., & Luria, A. R. (1928/1993). Etiudy pi. istorii povendeniia [Study on the history of behavior]. In *Studies on the history of behavior: Ape, primitive, and child* (pp. 3–11). Hillsdale, NJ: Erlbaum.

SECONDARY

Amman-Gainotti, M. (Ed). (1992, June). Contributions to the history of psychology. *Perceptual and Motor Skills, 74*(2), 1011–1015.

Andres, S. (1996). The unhistoric in history. *English Literary History, 26,* 79–95.

Balestra, D. J. (1980). The mind of Jean Piaget: Its philosophical roots. *Thought, 55,* 412–427.

Barrelet, J., & Perret-Clermont, A. (Eds.). (1996). *Jean Piaget et Neuchatel.* Lausanne, Switzerland: Payot.

Blanck, G. (1990). Vygotsky: The man and his cause. In L. Moll (Ed.), *Vygotsky and education.* New York: Cambridge Press.

Boden, M. (1979). *Jean Piaget.* NY: Viking Press.

Bovet, P. (1943). *La fondation et les quatre premieres annes (1893–1897) des Amis de la Nature.* Lecture given at the 15th anniversary of the Club of the Friends of Nature. Neuchatel, Switzerland: Delachaux & Nestle.

Bruner, J. (1957). *Contemporary approaches to cognition.* Cambridge, MA: Harvard University Press.

Bruner, J. (1967, Spring). *The Vygotsky memorial issue.* White Plains, NY: International Arts and Sciences Press.

Buissson, F. (1882). Club Jurassien. In F. Buisson (Ed.), *Dictionnaire de pedagogie et d'instruction primaire* (Vol. 1). Paris: Hachette.

Buscarlet, D. (1920). Notre inspiration. La Federation Universelle des Associations Chretiennes d'Etudiants. In *L'Association Chretienne d'Etudiants. Aux etudiants des universites.* Lausanne, Switzerland: La Concorde.

Carr, E. (1967). *What is history?* New York: Random House.

Chapman, M. (1988). *Constructive evolution.* New York: Cambridge University Press.

Cohen, L., Marion, L., & Morrison, K. (1989). *Research methods in education.* NY: Routledge.

Cohen, G.A. (1976). *Karl Marx's theory of history: A defense.* Oxford, UK: Oxford University Press.

Cole, M. (1996). *Culture in mind.* Cambridge, MA: Harvard University Press.

Cole, M. & Scribners. (1974). *Culture and thought: A psychological introduction.* NY: John Wiley.

Colet, N. R. (March 15, 1999). Personal communication.

Daniels, H. (Ed.). (1993). *Charting the agenda: Educational activity after Vygotsky.* London: Routledge.

Davydov, V. (1967). The problem of generalization in the works of L. S. Vygotsky. White Plains, NY: International Arts and Sciences Press.

Davydov, V., & Radzikhjovsky, L.A. (1985). Vygotsky's theory and the activity-oriented approach in psychology. In J. Wertsch (Ed.), *Culture, communication, and cognition.* Cambridge, UK: Cambridge University Press.

DeVries, R. (1997, March). Piaget's social theory. *Educational Researcher, 26,* 14–17.

Forman, G. (1980). In G. Garzda & R. Corsini (Eds.), *Theories of learning.* Itasca, IL: Peacock.

Gall, M., Borg, W., & Gall, J. (1996). *Educational research: An introduction.* White Plains, NY: Longman.

Gardiner, P. (1978). *The nature of historical explanations.* Oxford: Oxford University Press.

Gardner, J. (1996). The nature of leadership. In R. Greenleaf, D. Frick, & L. Spears (Eds.), *On becoming a servant-leader.* San Francisco: Jossey-Bass.

Gilbert, M. (1979) *The Jews of Russia.* Jerusalem: Bernstein.

Greenleaf, R., Frick, D., & Spears, L. (Eds.). *On becoming a servant-leader.* San Francisco, California: Jossey-Bass.

Gruber, H., & Vonche, J. (1995). *The essential Piaget.* New York: Basic Books.

Gredler, M. (1997). *Learning and instruction: Theory into practice.* Upper Saddle River, NJ: Merrill.

Hall, E. (1970). A conversation with Jean Piaget and Barbel Inhelder. *Psychology Today, 3,* 25–32, 54–56.

Hamilton, R. (1997, May). Lecture at the University of Houston on educational psychology.

Hardy, C. (1996). Beyond certainty: A personal odyssey. In R. Greenleaf, D. Frick, & L. Spears (Eds.), *On becoming a servant-leader.* San Francisco: Jossey-Bass.

Hill, J. E. & Kebert, A. (1967). *Models, methods, and analytical procedures in education and research.* Detroit, MI: Wayne State University Press.

Isaaca, N. (1974). *A brief introduction to Piaget.* New York: Schocken Books.

John-Steiner, V. (1985). *Notebooks of the mind.* Albuquerque: University of New Mexico Press.

Kagan, S. (2003). *Notes from Space.* Available: www.KaganOnline.com.

Kesselring, T. (1988). *Jean Piaget.* Munich: Verlag C. H. Beck.

Kozulin, A. (1991). *Vygotsky's psychology: A biography of ideas.* London: Harvester.

Kuhn, D. (1979, August). The application of Piaget's theory of cognitive development to education. *Harvard Educational Review, 49,* 340–360.

Leonard, B. (2003). Are you a standards-based teacher? *Science Teacher, 6*(2), 33–37.

Levitin, K. (1982). *One is not born a personality.* Moscow: Progress.

Meldvedev, R. A. (1974). *K sudu istorii. Genezis I posledstvija stalinizma.* New York: Knopf.

Modgil, S., Modgil, C., & Brown, G. (1983). *Jean Piaget: An interdisciplinary critique.* London: Routledge.

Montangero, J., & Maurice-Naville, D. (1997). *Piaget or the advance of knowledge.* London: Erlbaum.

Munari, A. (1994). Jean Piaget. *Prospects, 24,* 1–2, 311–327.

Newman, F., & Holzman, L. (1993). *Lev Vygotsky: revolutionary scientist.* New York: Routledge.

Newman, F. (Sepyember, 1995). *Who is L. S. Vygotsky?* Available: http://www.xmca-request@weber.ucsd.edu.

Nicolopoulou, A. (1993). Play, cognitive development, and the social world: Piaget, Vygotsky, and beyond. *Human Development, 36,* 1–23.

Pass, S. (April 21, 2003). Piaget and Vygotsky: Origination of their ideas. Paper presented at the American Educational Research Association. Chicago, IL.

Peterman, B. S. (1997). *Origins of Piaget's concept of decentration.* Houston, TX: CUS-Tos Press.

Piaget Group. (1996, May). *Information on Piaget* [Online]. Available: http://www.P540Piaget Group.

Pieron, H. (1966). Jean Piaget. *American Journal of Psychology, 79,* 147–150.

Pinkus, B. (1988). *The Jews of the Soviet Union. The history of a national minority.* Cambridge, UK: Cambridge University Press.

Prawat, R. (2002). Dewey and Vygotsky viewed through the rearview mirror—and dimly at that. *Educational Researcher. 31*(5), 16–20.

Prawat, R. (Fall, 2000) Dewey meets the "Mozart of Psychology" in Moscow: The untold story. *American Education Research Jurnal, 37*(3), 663–696.

Quinn, J., Mintzberg, H., & James, R. (1988). *The strategy process: Concepts, context, and cases.* Englewood Cliffs, NJ: Prentice Hall.

Ratner, C. (1991). *Vygotsky's sociohistorical psychology and its contemporary applications.* New York: Plenum Press.

Razmyslov, P. (1934). O kul'turno-istorichekoj teorii psikhologii. *Kniga I Proletarskaja Revoljucija, 4,* 78–86.

Rissom, I. (1985). *Der begriff des zeichens in den arbeiten lev semenovic Vygotskijs* [The lesson of the examples in the life of Lev Semenovic Vygotsky]. Gopingen, Germany: Kummerle Verlag.

Rothstein, B. (1998, June). Lecture at the John Ben Shepherd Institute.

Sants, P. (1983). Piaget's attitudes to education. In S. Modgil, C. Modgil, & G. Brown, *Jean Piaget: An interdisciplinary critique* (pp. 85–93). London: Routledge.

Schaeffer, T. (1982, September-October). The West Point thesis: Leadership through followership. *Business Horizons*, p. 3.

Slaughter, R. (1996). Long-term thinking and the politics of reconceptualization. *Futures, 28*, 75–86.

Smith, L. S. (1990). *Piaget, Vygotsky, and beyond*. NY: Routledge.

Smith, L. S. (1993). *Necessary knowledge*. London: Erlbaum.

Smith, L. S. (1995). Introduction. In J. Piaget, *Sociological studies*. London: Routledge.

Steffe, L., & Gale, J. (1995). *Constructivism in education*. Hillsdale, NJ: Erlbaum.

Sutton-Smith, B. (1979). *Play and learning*. New York: Gardner Press.

Steffe, L., & Gale, J. (1995). *Constructivism in education*. Hillsdale, NJ: Erlbaum.

Tuddenham, R. (1958). Jean Piaget and the world of the child. *American Psychologist, 21*(2), 207–212.

Tudge, J. & Winterhoff, P. (1993). Vygotsky, Piaget, and Bandera: Perspectives on the relationship between the social world and cognitive development. *Human Development, 36*, 61–81.

Tribolet, M. (1996). Portrait intellectuel et moral due pere de Jean Piaget. In J. Bartlett & Perret-Clermont (Eds.), *Jean Piaget et Neuchatel*. Lausanne: Payot.

Valsiner, J. (1988). *Developmental psychology in the Soviet Union*. Bloomington: Indiana University Press.

Van der Goot, M. (1989). *Piaget as a revolutionary thinker*. Bristol, IN: Wyndham Hall Press.

Van der Veer, R., & Valsiner, J. (1991). *Understanding Vygotsky*. Oxford, UK: Blackwell.

Vidal, F. (1989). Self and oeuvre in Jean Piaget's youth. In D. B. Wallace & H. E. Gruber (Eds.), *Creative people at work*. New York: Oxford University Press.

Vidal, F. (1994). *Piaget before Piaget*. Cambridge, MA: Harvard University Press.

The Vygotsky Group. (1996, August-October) *Information on Vygotsky* [Online]. Available: http.//www. P540Vygotsky Group.

Wertsch, J. V. (Ed.). (1981). *The concept of activity in Soviet psychology*. Armonk, NY: Sharpe.

Wertsch, J. V. (Ed.). (1985a). *Culture, communication, and cognition*. New York: Cambridge University Press.

Wertsch, J. V. (Ed.). (1985b). *Voice of the mind: A sociocultural approach to mediated action*. Cambridge, MA: Harvard University Press.

Wertsch, J. V. (1985c). *Vygotsky and the social formation of mind*. Cambridge, MA: Harvard University Press.

Wertsch, J. V. (1991) A sociocultural approach to socially shared cognition. In L. Resnick, J. Levine, & S. Teasley (Eds.), *Socially shared cognition* (pp.1–25). Washington DC: American Psychological Association.

Wertsch, J. V., & Tulviste, P. (1992). L. S. Vygotsky and contemporary developmental psychology. *Developmental Psychology, 28*(4), 548–557.

Yaroshevsky, M. G. (1994/1996). *History of psychology*. Moscow: Misl.

Yaroshevsky, M.G. (1996). *Vygotsky and his position on psychological sciences*. Orlando, FL: Paul M. Deutsch.

Zaporozhetz, A. (1967, Spring). *L. S. Vygotsky's role in the study of problems of perception*. White Plains, NY: Arts and Sciences Press.

APPENDIX

CHART 1: SIMILARITIES IN THE LIVES
OF PIAGET AND VYGOTSKY

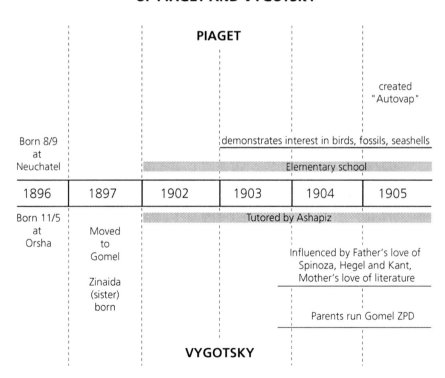

PIAGET

created "Autovap"

Born 8/9 at Neuchatel | demonstrates interest in birds, fossils, seashells

Elementary school

| 1896 | 1897 | 1902 | 1903 | 1904 | 1905 |

Born 11/5 at Orsha | Tutored by Ashapiz

Moved to Gomel

Zinaida (sister) born

Influenced by Father's love of Spinoza, Hegel and Kant, Mother's love of literature

Parents run Gomel ZPD

VYGOTSKY

Parallel Paths to Constructivism: Jean Piaget and Lev Vygotsky, pages 127–137
Copyright © 2004 by Information Age Publishing
127

PIAGET

Timeline (1906–1914):

1906 · "Our Birds"
- demonstrates interest in birds, fossils, seashells
- Elementary school

1907 · "Un Moineau Albionos"

1908 · Neuchatel Latin School
- volunteer: Neuchael Museum of Natural History

1909–1910

1911 · "Rameau de Sapin" articles on mollusks
- +Bedot offers him curator's job
- +Godet dies
- +finds Sabatier book in father's study
- +confirmation lessons
- First crisis: RELIGIOUS
- influenced by studying Bovet, Darwin, and Kant

1912 · *Cornut introduces him to Bergson
- member: Jura club
- member: Friends of Nature
- Neuchatel Latin School

1913 · *joins Swiss Natural Science Society and Association Chretienne Suisse d'Etudi
- *joins Swiss Zoological Society

1914 · WWI

VYGOTSKY

1906–1907 · Tutored by Ashapiz
- Influenced by Father's love of Spinoza, Hegel and Kant, Mother's love of literature

1908 · taught by Shipet
- +Bar mitzvah
- Parents run Gomel ZPD

1909 · Influenced by Father's love of Spinoza, Hegel and Kant, Mother's love of literature

1910 · forms his first ZPD in Gomel

1911 · Gymnasium
- Father tried and acquitted for defending Gomel during Czarist pogrom

1912 · Baccalaureate Gold Medal

1913 · Univ. of Moscow

1914 · Essay on 'Hamlet' · WWI

PIAGET

WORLD WAR I

1915	1916	1917	1918	1919	1920	1921	1922	1923

"The Mission of the Idea" "Recherere" "Language and Thought of Child"

*1st hopitalization in Swiss mtns. for nervous breakdown
*2nd hospitilization for nervous breakdown

influenced
member
member
sch.

Second crisis: PHILOSOPHICAL

Ph.D: Natural Sciences
ABD: Philosophy
Univ. of Neuchatel

Sabatier/Raymond Influence

Paris:
studies and works at Dr. Janet's lab.
studies and works at Lipps/Wrescher lab.
works at Bleuler's psychiatric clinic

+Works at Pierron's lab.
+Is given Binet's lab.
+Studies learning failures at Rue de la Grange aux Belles

+Semester at U. of Zurich studied psychology and psychoanalysis influenced by Freud

Sorbonne

*Tries to psychoanalyze his mother
*discovers his psycho-remembrance of a "kidnapping" when he was 8 was false

+rejects psychoanalysis

Research Director at Jean-Jacques Rousseau Institute at Geneva
Co-directorship with Claparede and Bovet leads to education commitment

*Marries Valentine Chatenay

VYGOTSKY

WORLD WAR I

University of Moscow (Medicine and Law)
Shanyavskii People's University (History and Philology) graduate of both

Teaches at Gomel public high school & teachers' college

+Tuberculosis diagnosed

RUSSIAN REVOLUTION
communism takes over

*Father heads Commercial Bank of Moscow

+Brother Dodik dies in Kiev

*Starts newspaper "Veresk"

*Runs Ages of Days Publishing Co.

runs second Gomel ZPD

PIAGET

1924	1925	1926	1927	1928	1929	1930	1931	1932

"Le Judgement et le raisonnement chex enfant" (1924)

Reads Vygotsky's "The Problem of the Cultural Development of the Child" (1924)

education commitment — Prof. of Psych., Soc, and the Phil. (1924)

+Daughter Jacqueline born (1925)

studies his own children (1925 →)

+Daughter Lucienne born (1927)

English publication of "Judgment and Reasoning in the Child" (1928)

Professor of History of Scientific Thought at University of Geneva (1929–1932)

+Son Laurent born (1931)

Read Vygotsky's "The Problem of the Cultural Development of the Child" (1932)

studies his own children (1932)

STALIN (1930–1932)

VYGOTSKY

+Lenin dies / Stalin grabs for power (1924)

Translates Piaget's 1923–24 books (1924)

+Daughter Gita Born (1924)

"Pedagogicheskaj and psikhlogija" (1924)

Reads Darwin, Piaget, etc. (1924)

Second troika with Luria and Leontiev for ZPDs in Moscow, Tashkent, and Kharkov (1924)

+1st hospitalization for tuberculosis (1924)

+Marries Rosa Noevna Smekova (1925)

+Addresses 2nd Psychological Congress (1925)

"Methodology of Reflexology and Psychological Studies" (1926)

Works at Moscow Kornilov Institute (1926)

Daughter Asya born (1927)

Director of Psych. Lab. for Abnormal Children (1927)

"Historical Meaning of the Crisis in Psychology" (1927)

Writes inrodution to translation of Piaget's 1923 "Language and Thought of the Child" (1927)

Second troika with Luria and Leontiev for ZPDs in Moscow, Tashkent, and Kharkov

"Problem of the Cultural Development of the Child" (1928)

+Stalin kills Kornilov (1929)

+Vygotsky goes into exile (1929)

+Stalin establishes dictatorship (1929)

Works for Psychological Institute outside of Moscow due to Stalin's purges / trains psychologists at 1st Central State U. in Tashkent

Reads Darwin, Piaget, etc. (1930)

"Study of Abnormal Behavior, Ape and Primitive Child" / "Struejur" (1930)

Department of Psychology at Ukranian Psychoneurological Institute at Kharkov volunteers with physically and mentally handicapped (1930–1932)

+Son born (1931)

works at finishing M.D. (1931)

"Lekeiipo psiklodogii" (1932)

"Rech i Myshlenie nebenka" (1932)

PIAGET

studies his own children

Honorary Doctorate Harvard

Professor of History of Scientific Thought at University of Geneva

Professor of Experimental Psychology at University of Geneva: 1940–71

Professor of Sociology at University of Georgia

Potessor of Experiemental Psychology and Sociology at University of Lausanne

1933	1934	1935	1936	1937	1938	1939	1940	1941

STALIN

VYGOTSKY

Department of Psychology at Ukranian Psychoneurological Institute at Kharkov volunteers with physically and mentally handicapped

+Stalin puts Vygotsky on trial for "political error"

Reads Darwin, Piaget, etc.

Second troika

Works Psychological Institute

1st Central State U.

Hospitalized for tuberculosis
Betrayal of Luria and Leontiev
Offered possibility of heading a section on Exp. Med. at All Union Institute of Exp. Med.
Tries to get "Thinking and Speech" smuggled out to Piaget

+Vygotsky dies before trial—June 11

PIAGET

"Traite de Logique" Honory Doctorate U. of Business Professor Honoris Causa U. of Brazil

"Introduction a la espitemologie genetique

Member Executive Council UNESCO

Professor of Experimental Psychology at University of Geneva: 1940–71

Professor of Sociology at University of Georgia

Pofessor of Experiemental Psychology and Sociology at University of Lausanne

| 1942 | 1943 | 1944 | 1945 | 1946 | 1947 | 1948 | 1949 | 1950 |

STALIN

VYGOTSKY

PIAGET

1951	1952	1953	1954	1955	1956	1957	1958	1959

Univ.Georgia

Lausanne

"Plays, Dreams, and Imitation in Childhood"

"Child's Conception of Number"

"Origins of Intelligence in the Child"

+Stalin dies

"Construction of Reality in the Child"

"Growth of Logical Thinking"

Professor of Experimental Psychology at University of Geneva: 1940–71

Director of International Center for Genetic Epistemology: 1955–80

Professor of Genetic Psychology at Sorbonne: 1952–63

STALIN

+Stalin dies

VYGOTSKY

PIAGET

Honorary Doctorate Cambridge

Writes commentary of Vygotsky's 1926 "Thinking and Speech"

"Logique et Connaissance scientifique"

Director of International Center for Genetic Epistemology: 1955–80

Professor of Experimental Psychology at University of Geneva: 1940–71

Professor of Genetic Psychology at Sorbonne: 1952–63

| 1960 | 1961 | 1962 | 1963 | 1964 | 1965 | 1966 | 1967 | 1968 |

VYGOTSKY

PIAGET

1969	1970	1971	1972	1973	1974	1975	1976	1977

Distinguished Scientific Contribution Award APA

University of Geneva

Honorary Doctorate U. of Bristol

"Biology and Knowledge"

Eresum Prize

"Main Trends in Psychology"

Director of International Center for Genetic Epistemology: 1955–80

Emeritus Professor at University of Geneva

"Recherches sur l'abstraction reflechissante"

Dir. Int'l Bureau of Education discovers socio-politcal issues in education

VYGOTSKY

PIAGET

"Intelligence
and Affectivity"
published
posthumously

+dies Sept 16

Director of International Center

University of Geneva

| 1978 | 1979–80 | 1981 |

VYGOTSKY

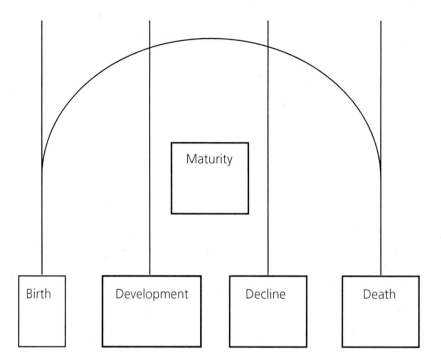

Factors of Influence During a LIfetime:
Political/Military • Economic • Social • Science/Technology
Religion • Philosophy • Arts/Education

Chart 2   The Curve

INDEX

Parallel Paths to Constructivism: Jean Piaget and Lev Vygotsky, pages 139–143
Copyright © 2004 by Information Age Publishing

Z

LaVergne, TN USA
26 May 2010

184064LV00002B/2/A